WEALTH CREATION

THE FOCUS

One of The Most Powerful Processes of Wealth Creation Without Question!

Rob Wilson

(Wealth Creation - The Focus)

ISBN 978-0-9721065-7-3

Printed in USA

Dedication

These series of Wealth Creation is dedicated to the many families that I have comes across in my work. It is also dedicated to you the now reader, whether you are reading just this book or the entire series, I am in prayer that you experience wealth creation personally.

I especially wish that you who have chosen to read this series find what they are seeking.

To: Pastor Allen

Rob Wilson

5/21/23

Focus require commitment, commitment is best done when you know your purpose. It's what inspires you while taking action.

Table of Contents

Foreword

A well-known Bible scripture and favorite of mine is found in the Book of Amos, chapter 3, verse 3: "Can two walk together, unless they are agreed." (NKJV)

One might wonder, how does this verse relate to Rob's Wealth Creation Mindset? The answer is simple. Whatever you FOCUS on daily, will significantly impact if not fully determine your life's outcome. In other words, your FOCUS and your DAILY ACTIVITIES must agree / align for you to achieve your wealth creation goals.

In this forth book series on Wealth Creation, Rob masterfully lays out what I call "FOCUS Busters" and "FOCUS Builders". He artfully says, "show me a person's day and I'll tell you to a high degree of certainty what their wealth-building future looks like."

To that point, I have had the pleasure of knowing Rob for over 10 years. Several of those years were up close and intimate as I sat, watched, and listened to him lead a flock of followers who were attempting to grow their financial portfolios; seemingly desiring overnight success.

One of the things that I've admired most about Rob is his honest and direct communications that Wealth Creation is not an overnight reality, but instead, accomplished over time, and to be successful over time, not only in wealth creation, but also professionally, personally, physically, in marriage, family and in faith, it requires FOCUS.

Unwavering FOCUS. It is under Rob's tutelage many of us have learned albeit during reflection moments, that whatever is acquired fast, often leaves us, even faster!

So, as you read Wealth Creation – The FOCUS, allow Rob to help you uncover those things you personally do to hinder your success in creating wealth for self and for the legacy you hope to leave for generations that come after you.

Remember, "We are what we repeatedly do. Excellence, then, is not an act but a habit." Will Durant

Are you a procrastinator, content with where you are in life or live in a world of false expectations?

Wealth Creation – The FOCUS will help you find Purpose and Direction.

It is not the swift who succeed, but those that don't quit nor lose their FOCUS of the dream. Enjoy the Journey and stay FOCUSED!

- LaMonte Jones – Business Advisor

Preface

I want YOU the reader to develop a focus-based approach that you can use to achieve your personal and financial goals through daily practical exercises and habits that you can implement into your daily life to actively shape your wealth creation future.

So many times you have set goals for yourself, feeling determined and confident, thinking that there is nothing that can stop you from achieving them.

Later, when the momentum passes and the initial motivation starts to fade, it seems that there is something that can indeed stand in your way: YOU are that thing. Isn't that frustrating?

I recently talked with a dear friend and she was telling me how she has a focus-based approach after going over what you will learn in this book. Two years ago prior to learning these principles she was on a weight loss journey.

Her goal was to lose 54 pounds in 90 days, well with all of her effort by day 35 she had completely abandoned that goal. Now, using the focus-based approach, she has successfully lost 58 pounds in 190 days.

So many people start businesses or personal journeys to achieve a change, such as losing weight but give up on the way.

This is the result of an unfocused mindset. You expect your motivation to last through to the end of your endeavors, but fail to realize that the initial determination is just the spark that sets things in motion.

Along the way, many obstacles will show, and only a focused mind will be able to overcome them and reach the desired goal. Establishing successful habits and actively focusing on the small, daily things that you do is the change factor. To shape our future, you must first shape your present.

Introduction

First, let me think of the number of things that I have done without focusing. It is just too many. In fact I am amazed by the number of things that I have done well and accomplished. All of it without having focus. Indulge me for a moment and think about yourself, the things that you have done and accomplished without really focusing on those things.

Wait, I hear people now saying how it had to be some form of focusing in order for you, me, them or anyone else to have done a single thing. I will agree just a little, maybe a little more. You see, for me, many of the things that I did or accomplished were things that I started and was okay with the end results.

It was things that I came to take or leave. Have you ever heard people say it is what it is? So what is the point of putting energy behind it is what it is. Wealth Creation is purpose driven, it is not "it is what it is". Your health is purpose driven, it is not "it is what it is". We can go on and on about what it is and what it is not.

This is why I am writing this book of The Wealth Creation Series The Focus, it's purposeful, it's another part of the bigger vision inside of you who are reading this series. Some may not get this, I really would hate to learn that this and the other books are just a good read. I am writing for impact. I want to change your life forever.

Oh back to thinking, I hope by now you realize that there are a few things in your life that you really never apply focus to. It did not hurt you in any way or did it? Were you able to fully succeed on whatever it was that you did without really focusing? Could you have accomplished more if you would have focused on it?

Listen, your focus must be targeted, you now must open your vision wider so that you understand what is necessary for you to accomplish any and all wealth creation goals. If you are like me and most people, we consider ourselves workaholics, we love what we do. It's so easy to get in the work mode and stay there because we truly love the work we do. Okay most of us.

Yet – and this is the dark side of being a workaholic – it's very easy to get busy and focus our attention on tasks that aren't that important – they don't help you finish, and they help you finish a task, but not the task you should be working on.

It's easy to get caught up in busyness, you see this is one of your mindset blind spots. This is one of the biggest turning points on this wealth creation journey by realizing that busyness can be a form of procrastination and you are not really focused.

The Focus

Chapter 1

Procrastination

Focus is the cure of many things, as you will learn in this book focus may be the most powerful aspect of the Wealth Creation series. I do not care about the mindset, without focus it's nothing more than a thought. I do not care about the influencer, it too is simply nothing without a dose of focus.

Please remember this.

Yes Focus is the cure to your procrastination, lack of direction, and productivity. By applying the advice from the book, you can overcome the things that keep you from achieving your objectives and become so committed to wealth creation. It all starts with a focused mind. I will talk about how you can achieve that.

But first, let's look at these things for what it is. It affects your savings and investing, actually it affects your basic planning process. You see procrastination is the act of delaying or putting off tasks until the last minute, or past their deadline.

Even with known potentially negative consequences ahead of you, your irrational delay of tasks is nothing but a form of self-regulation with failure all over it. No matter how well-organized and committed you are, chances are that you have found yourself frittering away hours on trivial pursuits (watching TV, updating your Facebook status, shopping online) when you should have been spending that time on planning and mapping out your finances for wealth creation or work-related projects.

We all are guilty of putting off finishing a project, avoiding work assignments, or ignoring household chores, all procrastination will have a major impact on your job, your career, and your life.

Let’s be clear, procrastination is not a sign of a serious problem. It's a common tendency that most people give in to at some point or another.

I want you to really have a focus-based approach about your financial future. This procrastination stuff is huge, I need for you to get out of your way. There are these things that always seem to remind you that you got this when you don’t.

Hey, remember that time that you thought you had a week left to finish a project that was really due the next day? How about the time you decided not to clean up your apartment because you "didn't feel like doing it right now?" oh and then a guest shows up at your door.

We often assume that projects won't take as long to finish as they really will, which can lead to a false sense of security when we believe that we still have plenty of time to complete it.

One of your biggest factors contributing to procrastination is the notion that you have to feel inspired or motivated to earn money, save money and invest money at a particular moment.

The reality is that if you wait until you're in the right frame of mind to do certain tasks (especially undesirable ones), you will probably find that the right time simply never comes along and the task never gets completed.

Work with me here, how many times have you looked at the money you have earned and decided that you were going to start investing? Now maybe just maybe you are realizing you have been overestimating how much time you have left to perform a task.

Do not find yourself guilty of overestimating how motivated you will be in the future. Then find yourself underestimating how long certain activities will take to complete. Oh my, I don't want to do this, it's going to take forever.

And now, mistakenly assume that you need to be in the right frame of mind to start wealth creation or have a certain amount of money.There is something out there about "Present Bias Procrastination" which simply means you are human. LOL...

Instant gratification causes you to procrastinate and seems to motivate you slightly for immediate gratification or rewards than by long-term rewards.

Looking at it this way, the immediate reward of staying in bed and watching TV is more appealing than the long-term reward of sitting down mapping out an investment strategy, which would take much longer to accomplish.

This is why it feels so good to procrastinate. This is also why wealth creation is delayed and denied. You may not like me to bring up depression, hopelessness and all of that negative stuff I wrote about in the mindset.

But you have to understand that in order for you to master focusing on your wealth creation you need to understand the killers, the road blocks that seem like nothing. Be it known that procrastination can also be a result of depression. Feelings of hopelessness, helplessness, and a lack of energy can make it difficult to start (and finish) the simplest things.

Depression can also lead to self-doubt. When you can't figure out how to tackle your financial goals or feel insecure about your abilities, you might find it easier to put it off.

There are a few things that I also think are pretty common in people: fears about making new mistakes, doubts about doing something correctly, and worry over others' expectations. If you are constantly finding yourself being indecisive, you now know that will cause you to procrastinate rather than making a decision.

Poor people, yes, poor people always seem to come up with reasons and excuses about why they cannot get things done due to procrastination.

- Not feeling in the mood to do it
- Being in the habit of waiting until the last minute
- Believing that you work better under pressure

- Thinking that you can finish it at the last minute
- Waiting for the right moment
- Needing time to think about the task

This is a poverty mindset all day long with these types of excuses. I have to be completely transparent here. I used to use a few of these excuses daily for a large part of my life. Sad but true, and if you are honest you may very well say me too.

Okay, this is getting deep, even for me as a writer. If you really get how harmful and subtle procrastination is in the cycle of your life you would begin to make many changes, forget wealth creation.

Check this out, there are two types of procrastinators: Passive and Active procrastinators. YEP!!

Passive Procrastinators: Delay the task because they have trouble making decisions and acting on them

Active procrastinators: Delay the task purposefully because working under pressure allows them to "feel challenged and motivated"

- Perfectionist – Puts off tasks out of the fear of not being able to complete a task perfectly
- Dreamer – Puts off tasks because they are not good at paying attention to detail
- Defier - Doesn't believe someone should dictate their time schedule

- Worrier – Puts off tasks out of fear of change or leaving the comfort of "the known"
- Crisis-maker – Puts off tasks because they like working under pressure
- Overdoer – Takes on too much and struggles with finding time to start and complete task

There are non-procrastinators who focus on the goals that they have. They have a stronger personal identity and are less concerned about what or how others like them.

People who don't procrastinate tend to be high in the personality trait known as conscientiousness. People who are high in conscientiousness also tend to be high in other areas including self-discipline, persistence, and personal responsibility.

It is only in cases where procrastination becomes chronic and begins to have a serious impact on a person's daily life that it becomes a more serious issue. In such instances, it's not just a matter of having poor time management skills, it's a major part of their lifestyle.

Unfortunately, this procrastination can have a serious impact on a number of life areas, including a person's mental health and social, professional, and financial well-being. Also fortunately, there are a number of different things you can do to fight procrastination and start getting things done on time.

This series is about helping you to develop wealth creation that will last for generations. As I suggest that you develop a schedule, carefully plan your financial tasks, and improve your time-management skills, you will discover effective ways to cope with procrastination.

Much of the design necessary that will keep you on schedule you should have already read in The Mindset. However I am going to give you ways to deal directly with some of the main causes of procrastination. Deal with Your Fear

Fear is one factor that contributes to procrastination. This can involve a fear of failure, a fear of making mistakes, or even a fear of success. Listen, as I am writing this series I am overcoming fear of success. I have carried this fear for almost my entire career as a financial coach.

- Who's going to believe me?
- Why did God gift me in this area?
- I come from a poverty background?

If you are afraid of success because you secretly believe that you don't deserve it, it is important to realize that your self-handicapping might be keeping you from achieving your goals. By addressing the fear that is keeping you from getting started head on, you can begin to overcome your procrastination habit.

Some many people are earning the income, living what can be described as your best life and still unable to get beyond their fears to have the successful life that they truly desire. One's best life can only be a level above poverty and they are happy with that.

You have to start by creating a to-do list with things that you would like to accomplish. If necessary, put a date next to each item if there is a deadline that you need to meet.

I know this sounds like the same old things to do, but remember there are two purposes here. Wealth Creation for generation and the focus necessary to meet that goal are your purposes.

When you are saving and investing it is not difficult to determine the amount that you will use weekly or monthly, it's the return that you will receive.

So when you are trying to set estimates on how long each goal will take to complete, be realistic, and then double that number so that you don't fall into the cognitive trap of underestimating how long each goal will take.

When you are faced with hard times, you might feel daunted, intimidated, or even hopeless when you look at the sheer amount of effort required. At this point, take individual items on your list and break them down into a series of steps. Much like I am doing with this series.

If you need to create a budget first, what steps do you need to follow? If you are planning a big family event, what are the things you need to do and what supplies do you need to obtain?

Once you have created a list detailing the process you need to go through in order to accomplish your goals, you can start working on individual "intentional steps."

As you start to tackle items on your list, pay attention to when thoughts of procrastination start to creep into your mind. If you find yourself thinking "I don't feel like doing this now" or "I'll have time to work on this later," then you need to recognize that you are about to procrastinate.

When you feel tempted to procrastinate, don't give in to the urge. Instead, force yourself to spend at least a few minutes working on your vision. You might discover that it is easier to complete once you get started.

It's hard to get any real results when you keep turning your attention to what's on television or you keep checking your friends' Facebook status updates.

Assign yourself a period of time during which you turn off all distractions—such as music, television, and social networking sites—and use that time to focus all of your attention on wealth creation.

Once you have completed a goal (or even a small portion of a larger goal), it is important to reward yourself for your efforts. Reward does not mean to sabotage your efforts or purposes with the mentality of I deserve this.

It's okay to give yourself the opportunity to indulge in something that you find fun and enjoyable, whether it's attending a sporting event, playing a video game, watching your favorite TV show, or looking at pictures on a social sharing site.

Procrastination

Breaking the procrastination habit isn't easy. The urge to put things off can be strong, especially when there are so many things around you to provide fun and entertaining distractions.

While procrastination might not be something you can avoid entirely, becoming cognizant of the reasons why you procrastinate and how to overcome those tendencies can help. By implementing these strategies, you might find that it is easier to put your nose to the grindstone and get started on those wealth creation goals.

For each statement below, circle the answer that most applies to rate yourself by indicating the extent to which each statement is characteristic or uncharacteristic of you.

The scale ranges from (1) 'Not like me at all' to (5) 'Very like me.' Note that (3) on the scale is neutral i.e. the statement is neither characteristic nor uncharacteristic of you. Calculate Your Total to add up your score and check your result using the scoring table underneath.

15 Statements to Answer

1. I often find myself performing tasks that I had intended to do days before.

(1) Not like me at all (2) Not like me (3) Neither like me or not (4) Like me (5) Very like me

2. When planning a meeting, I make the necessary arrangements well in advance.

(1) Not like me at all (2) Not like me (3) Neither like me or not (4) Like me (5) Very like me

3. I generally return emails and phone calls promptly.

(1) Not like me at all (2) Not like me (3) Neither like me or not (4) Like me (5) Very like me

4. I find that jobs often don't get done for days, even when they require little else except sitting down and doing them.

(1) Not like me at all (2) Not like me (3) Neither like me or not (4) Like me (5) Very like me

5. Once I have the information I need, I usually make decisions as soon as possible.

(1) Not like me at all (2) Not like me (3) Neither like me or not (4) Like me (5) Very like me

6. When I have something difficult to do, I tell myself that it's better to wait to do it until I'm feeling more inspired.

(1) Not like me at all (2) Not like me (3) Neither like me or not (4) Like me (5) Very like me

7. I usually have to rush to complete tasks on time.

(1) Not like me at all (2) Not like me (3) Neither like me or not (4) Like me (5) Very like me

8. I usually accomplish all the things I plan to do in a day.

(1) Not like me at all (2) Not like me (3) Neither like me or not (4) Like me (5) Very like me

9. I usually start a task I'm given shortly after I'm given it.

(1) Not like me at all (2) Not like me (3) Neither like me or not (4) Like me (5) Very like me

10. When deadlines are approaching, I often waste time by doing other things.

(1) Not like me at all (2) Not like me (3) Neither like me or not (4) Like me (5) Very like me

11. I often have a task finished sooner than necessary.

(1) Not like me at all (2) Not like me (3) Neither like me or not (4) Like me (5) Very like me

12. When preparing for a meeting, I am seldom caught having to do something at the last minute.

(1) Not like me at all (2) Not like me (3) Neither like me or not (4) Like me (5) Very like me

13. I often delay starting tasks that I have to do.

(1) Not like me at all (2) Not like me (3) Neither like me or not (4) Like me (5) Very like me

14. When faced with a huge task, I figure out what the first step is so that I can get going.

(1) Not like me at all (2) Not like me (3) Neither like me or not (4) Like me (5) Very like me

15. I frequently say "I'll do it tomorrow".

(1) Not like me at all (2) Not like me (3) Neither like me or not (4) Like me (5) Very like me

Calculate Your Total = 0

Score Interpretation Score & Comment

15-30

You're a procrastinator, and it's not something to be proud of. It means that you miss deadlines and waste a lot of time. As a result, your boss is not getting from you what you're capable of delivering, and he or she is probably very frustrated with this.

31-45

You're a mild procrastinator. You need to understand better why you procrastinate - there are several reasons for it, and more than one may apply to you. And you need to learn the steps you can take to stop doing it.

46-75

Good news! You're not a systematic procrastinator! If you do, however, occasionally catch yourself procrastinating over something.

Chapter Two

Contentment

Why contentment usually does not lead to happiness. There is a story that I remember being told when I was younger. It seems to have a number of different meanings and versions of the story. However, I want to try and establish that contentment can be a problem.

There was a man of deep faith who believed and trusted God completely in everything. One day the weather took a turn for the worse and the forecasters were calling for an evacuation to the city. It announced there would be great flooding and land erosion.

This gentleman lives in an area that was elevated (Higher than others) so he was content being in that space. As he stood outside observing the thousands of people fighting to evacuate and move to higher ground he was content with his position and his faith.

As the water begins to flood his home, people running by ask him to join them and save himself. His reply was "May God Will Provide", not long after as the water got higher some in a canoe came by and said I have room get in and save yourself.

Again, his reply "May God Will Provide", then a speed boat came by as this man was on the second floor of his home and they called out to him come on man save yourself.

Yet, this man is firm with his faith replies "May God Will Provide", let me remind you the scope of this flooding is massive. He was warned that this would be a great flood and yet he decided to remain where he was with his comforts and his faith.

Then as he made his way to the roof of his home and the water continued to rise there was a larger boat much like a yacht calling out to him save yourself, save yourself this may be your last chance. As the rain begins to overtake him he still was able to reply "May God Will Provide", just as he drowns.

He is now dead, standing before God, full of questions about his journey and why he was not saved by Him. His conversation with God:

Him – God I have always trusted you.
God – I know, and for that I continually blessed you.
Him – I stood on my faith in you
God – I sent you a news broadcast of bad weather coming.
Him – Yes, I trusted that you would save me
God – I tried, I sent people walk, running warning you
Him – You never fail me before, I trusted
God – I sent some in canoe to warn you
Him – I have done the right thing while believing in you
God – This I know and I sent a speed boat to get you.
Him – I was steadfast, trusting and having faith in you.
God – I am your God, I sent you everything you needed to say to yourself and you were content with what you had known and you missed all of my efforts to take you to a higher level.

His experience of staying in one place should teach all of us that "people who moved" and those who didn't perished. "Movement is life".

To be content is to perish. There is no "middle ground" which you can occupy, to simply settle where you are diminishes your growth. You must either go forward or fall behind: to stand still is impossible.

I believe that contentment is an enemy of your focus. I want you to be able to see why you cannot be content; why you can only surge ahead or collapse. Yet, most people do not see how this same principle works. In fact, we are taught that contentment is a big virtue, that it is a state of satisfaction attained with some success.

After all our reasonable material needs are fulfilled, we are told, we must not yearn for more and more. Contentment is stillness, it is peace, and it is stability. It is a nicer word for falling behind. If ambition is a capacity for unhappiness, contentment is the talent for happiness.

Maybe because I grew up poor, I have known many content types. I myself was one once, but then the zombies came for me. I refused to be dead.

I have known people who have escaped their circumstances through hard work and then grown content. People who have gotten a great break in their lives and embraced a peaceful life of not wanting more than a comfortable life.

Contentment

Most of them are bitter today. Contentment, it turns out, does not lead to happiness.

When it comes down to wealth creation you must have a focus to accumulate wealth. If you are not moving forward towards it, you are slipping backwards.

Contentment may have a middle ground. The very poor cannot possess it. It emerges from a material state that is not very low. As the content stays still, others around them prosper. There are lessons to be learned. Prosperity is inflationary to wealth creation.

Some could say defining the quality of the content types is bitterness. You could be both content and successful at the same time. So you think your happiness may emerge from your contentment. In reality, it emerged from superficial success.

Listen, if you remain still, you rot. If you do not have ambitions, you can be destroyed by a sudden phenomenon, like a pandemic. But then should the fear of destruction change your character?

The problem is not in the scale of success or even the devaluation of the middle ground. Contentment is bliss, so long as the people who have it also have the humor to tolerate being overtaken by the restless. Those who refuse to remain still.

Remember here I am talking about how contentment is an enemy to your ability to focus to create wealth. Focus has a few sources of enemies that we often become complacent with in our day to day lives that we are unable to recognize the damage it causes.

I must go here because many of my readers will be questioning why I did not incorporate the spiritual aspect of this thing called contentment. This is the listen, regardless of your faith or lack thereof, this is my strongest argument that contentment is a problem towards wealth creation.

Why is contentment a problem?

Biblically, when you consider the principles of the bible it is speaking in terms of godly character. As with most aspects of godly character, contentment is a middle path between two unacceptable extremes, complacency and covetousness.

In this world contentment is rare–more and more people are rarely satisfied with their relationships, with their possessions, with their place in life.

We are complacent when it comes to our morals–not often diligent in fulfilling our duties, or we are greedy when it comes to desiring more power and money and higher positions for ourselves.

Even this greediness has absolutely nothing to do with our desire for wealth creation. But though we often waver between complacency and covetousness, we seldom find contentment much less remain there for any length of time.

Contentment can very well be considered as an active state, though it is often portrayed passively. I say portrayed passively. I think of many clients and people I know who are so content with their life and have been for years that they have never left the environment that they grew up in.

I mean that they are still living within 200 yards of where they grew up, 40 plus years in the same apartment complex or government housing. They are still passively paying rent, living a very complacent life desiring nothing more.

Biblically, it is an active satisfaction with what God has given in blessings and the ability to create wealth, taking those steps as is necessary to fulfill the responsibilities that you have.

You must do things while resisting both the urge to coast and to fail to give your best. Think about it this way, you remain patient for God to fulfill our deepest and unmet longings.

You believe that he will supply your every need. You become good stewards with the things he has provided, you are coasting through, and you are not pushing to have or be more. There is this fear of the enemy.

There are many enemies to contentment but they generally boil down to one of two larger categories: complacency or covetousness.

Each of these can be a serious enemy to genuine contentment–one because it places undue stress on others for your free riding and failure to behave responsibly, and the other because it places pressure on your relationships with others and your stability because of your desire for more than what you do not possess, which can lead you to neglect to appreciate those things that you do have.

In fact, these two enemies are in reality often mirroring images of each other, and sometimes both present the same problems.

How can you focus on wealth creation when you are in a consistent battle with yourself about yourself?

You are trying not to be a freeloader, not wanting to seem that you are better than someone in your circle just because you want something different, something more.

I hate to say this, but it is especially frustrating when encountering people that are complacent about themselves but try to nag you and others into doing more.

For example, when people demand that other people cut them a lot of slack because of health problems or age or other factors but are not willing to cut the same amount of slack for others, there is a serious problem.

The same is true when others demand to be forgiven of their mistakes but are not willing to do the same for others either. What we have here are failures in respect and reciprocity that make genuine relationships impossible.

The same is true in reverse.

If you are not careful you can become poisoned with ambition and desire to climb the ladder to reach the height of your ambitions but might expect your partner to be content with the little time that you can give them and with less desirable tasks because of your ambition.

Again we can see clearly that this can be toxic to you focusing on wealth creation and generational wealth. You are not supposed to become this poisoned person.

This is also a failure of reciprocity, desiring the benefits of ambition and covetousness for yourself while being complacent about the state of your relationships and desiring all of the work for stability and contentment to come from others as a free benefit to you. Do not let respect become lacking towards others.

What many do not understand about contentment is it is so hard and it requires a lot of effort and its benefits tend to be back-loaded. Most people are oriented to working with short-term time frames.

Success is wanted immediately and quickly–and those tasks (Wealth Creation) that do not offer instant gratification of some kind tend to get neglected as unsatisfying, regardless of how important and necessary they are.

One of the biggest challenges I am faced with is that many of my students and clients are generally unwilling to pay and suffer now for benefits later on.

This disproportionately between one's inability either to wait for benefits or accept present suffering in exchange for future glory tends to reinforce only a very small amount of behaviors that are generally not productive over the long run.

But, with this mindset, future values tend to be discounted to zero anyway, so the long run is not even taken into consideration. I am not talking about a raise on your job, a credit score that allows you to get a good loan on your car or a house.

I am not talking about your yearly vacation or rental property, nor am I talking about your 401K plan. Wealth creation is much larger than this space that will trap you.

Both covetousness and complacency are short-term oriented strategies. Complacency is the strategy we operate when we do not want to think about future suffering so we put it out of mind by not worrying about problems or dealing with them before it is absolutely necessary and we are forced to wrestle with them.

Covetousness is our look for short-term benefits (especially from what others possess or what we do not have) without an eye toward long-term sustainability or viability.

One strategy focuses on our desire to avoid suffering and unpleasantness, and the other on our desire for results now without being patient for steady long-term growth.

And both tend to result in bad long-term results–burnout, broken relationships, mistrust and skepticism over repeated false promises. Broke, bankruptcy, all kinds of hardship, not to mention a poverty mindset.

So, contentment is a problem and not just with your ability to focus. It is hard to be you when other people do not appreciate how difficult those tasks are to accomplish. It is hard to remain content and not succumb to envy when you see other people enjoy your deepest longings and see no way for you to enjoy those anytime soon.

It is hard to trust that God will fulfill His promises when you are used to other people not meeting their duties and responsibilities in the past. It is hard to be good when evil seems to prosper for now. It is hard to work hard and be patient when no results seem forthcoming.

Contentment

No one said contentment was easy–the real question is whether it is worth it, when viewed over the long run. See you can invest today and nothing happens, you continue and again nothing happens so you are ready to abandon the process because you see a knucklehead who just threw money in the market and just like that they are seemingly winning.

Again, I am assuming that I am dealing with readers who are genuinely hard working and value relationships and are trustworthy people of integrity, is it better to be patient? Absolutely.

Is it better for you to accept your strengths and weaknesses and to work toward minimizing the weaknesses and maximizing the strengths, whether you are in businesses or governments or families or churches? Absolutely.

But, you have to make sure that you are neither too covetous nor pushy for yourself (or too nagging of others) or too complacent about yourself and your efforts.

That is the real difficulty of contentment, the real problem you have to deal with. Balance is always difficult to attain and even more difficult to maintain in the face of pressures in many directions. What was satisfactory in your past may not be in your present, and certainly will not be in your future.

Some growth is expected over time, and as a result, your contentment tends to mean that requirements are scaled to grow at a steady and gradual rate, not so fast that it requires shortcuts and leads to burnout, and not nonexistent so that you become lazy and complacent.

Rather, your goal is to be pokey turtles moving little by little in the right direction, consolidating your gains, and then moving on to further challenges while remaining content with what

God has given you for now, in the hope that you will receive the blessings and objects of your longing if you remain patient, hardworking and focus.

I believe that one of your biggest influencers is yourself. However, I accept the fact that there are many other parts to the process. Wealth creation is a mission, it's a desire that is nested in the heart of the discoverer. Wealth Creation is the balance of three things, the mind, the heart and your action.

Contentment does not mean lowering our expectations and bracing ourselves for hardship. But it does mean learning to accept that trials, pain, and suffering are all a part of our lives and can be used to teach us, make us strong.

As you move forward, understand that contentment refers to the state or feeling of being satisfied with what one is or has, not wanting more or anything else, while expectation means an expectant mental attitude and happiness refers to the quality or state of being happy or good fortune, pleasure, contentment or joy.

As I wrap this up, how many people actually experience contentment? How many actually feel satisfied with what you have? How many of you are still looking for better things despite having good things already?

Sometimes we are too focused on achieving something that is so superficial that we forget that deep down, the reason for wanting it - to feel contentment and satisfaction.

But we begin to lose that feeling when we keep "chasing" and "working" for it and later find out that there are better ones than the one that we had chased. Then what?

We continue to chase and chase..... and there will never be the end.

Chapter Three

Expectation

You want to acquire wealth, lots of wealth maybe. Wealth creation can simply be your expectation for yourself as you move forward. So will/should you set or have expectations? Will expectations set you up for failure, heartache, frustration, suffering, and disappointment – something pretty much so about 99.9% of the time.

Is the secret to a blissful life really as easy as letting go of your expectations? Some may think that it is at least a big step in the right direction on your path to wealth creation. But how do you let go of expectations when the very idea has been ingrained in our minds since... Well, forever? Expectation can be a powerful asset to your ability to focus.

At some point in your life, you may get tired of all the disappointments and your heart being broken because what you expected didn't come to fruition.

After a lot of reflection and hard work (and it still is hard work!), you tried your absolute best to not have expectations. You tried to let things be, as the pieces may fall where they will.

I am not going to say each of you have the same level of expectations, but it is something that requires your understanding. You may want to slap yourself when you have an expectation that keeps letting you down. Let's not get this twisted.

Expectation

Yes, expectations have let many, if not most people down. But you need to consider what expectations are. It is a want, a desire, a belief, or emotional anticipation you have about a future vision of yourself, an event, or action.

The future belief can be short term (5 minutes or a day from now), medium term (a week or a month from now), or long term (years from now).

I tell my clients often that you do have to be careful because expectations can also be realistic or unrealistic, and it's usually the "pie in the sky," "airy-fairy" expectations that cause us hurt, suffering, and frustration. It is the unrealistic side of your expectations that brings pain.

When you have expectations about anything – yourself, your friends and family, wealth creation, or life in general. Having an expectation is like having a wannabe reality you look forward to manifesting and actualizing.

An example of a realistic expectation would be that you expect to start a new job on November 3rd because that's what the date on your contract with your new employer states. This expectation is like an agreement between you and your boss – you both agreed on your starting date.

Another example is you agreeing to owning shares of a particular stock every single month. With this investment you agree to never withdraw or sell any shares. Your expectation is the wealth you created allows this to fall into place with the commitment of $100 a month.

On the other hand, before I give you an example of an unrealistic expectation, let's look at this way for clarity. They are rigid. They don't leave room for changing circumstances or allow you or others to be flexible.

Sometimes the expectations might seem reasonable, fair, and realistic, but your experience reveals they can't be met. Your expectations can also create more problems than they solve.

There's only one person in this world you can truly change—yourself—and even that takes a tremendous amount of effort. The only way that people change is through the desire and wherewithal to change themselves.

Still, it's tempting to try to change someone who doesn't want to change, as if your sheer will and desire for them to improve will change them (as it has you). You might even actively choose people with problems, thinking that you can "fix" them. Let go of this faulty expectation. Build your life around genuine, positive people, and avoid problematic people that bring you down.

When you expect things, you believe that something will happen in one way, but things don't always go according to our plans, or you expected more than what was realistically possible. When the expectation doesn't become reality, you feel disappointment and eventually even resentment.

Expectation

This should not be hard to believe that most people do not expect to ever experience financial freedom or wealth creation. Their financial lives are caught with earning six figures and living their best life. Whatever that is for them, this should not be you after these Wealth Creation books.

One of my mentors once explained to me the power of unmet expectations is so significant – it negatively impacts how we see ourselves, the people around us, and the world.

Having expectations (aka premeditated resentments) leads you down the road of disappointments. But why do we have expectations in the first place? Are they something we learn? Are they something we intrinsically have?

Expectations are rooted in experiences you have with:

Yourself
Your folks
Your family
Your friends
Your peers and colleagues
Your mentors
Media and society

It feels like you are programmed to have (and live up to) expectations. Past experiences all teach us a few things, and one of these lessons is to form expectations. For example, I have a "family" who only ever talked to me when they wanted something. Repeated exposure to this behavior has taught me to expect that they wanted something when they called me.

Expectations are really rooted in how you think about things. It's always a good idea to journal about your expectations so you can become consciously aware of the expectations you have.

Expectations are not the same as having goals or aspirations. Goals are intentional and achievable.

You work toward a goal you have to make it come true. The outcome of a goal is predictable, and you can make adjustments on your journey to the goal destination. An expectation is merely a perception (and desire and maybe false hope) that something will turn out a certain way; it's generally ambiguous and possible but not probable.

It's essential to note that not all expectations are bad. It's the unrealistic expectations and the too high expectations that trip you up, setting you up for failure. We falsely believe that having expectations results in happiness when the future wants or belief is fulfilled. But in reality, the happiness equation looks more like:

Happiness = Reality – Expectations

The effects of too high and unrealistic expectations are many. These kinds of expectations:

1. Set you up for failure when the expectation you have isn't met
2. Destroy your sense of self when you continuously try to rise and meet the expectations of others
3. Damage your relationships with other people when they don't live up to the expectations you have of who they are, how they should act and behave, and what they should do
4. Result in feeling disappointed, stressed, discouraged, and heart sore, and it builds resentment
5. Make you feel less than and not worthy or good enough when you don't meet and surpass expectations you have of yourself or the expectations others have of you
6. Prevent you from being happy as you feel disappointed in yourself and the people around you
7. Make you tired and feel run down

When you have (too high) expectations, you feel like you have a sense of control over your future, but in essence, it's merely an illusion. Goals are something you can control; expectations aren't.

Danger! Warning Signs You Should Let Go of Your Expectations

Several warning signs that it's definitely time for you to let go of expectations are when:

1. Little things set you off
2. You often feel let down by others or that you let yourself down
3. You take your perfectionistic tendencies to a whole new level and obsess over the minutest of details
4. You have detailed "checklists" (aka, expectations) for almost every aspect of your life
5. The people in your life call you a perfectionist or say you are too critical
6. You often feel guilty (when you expect too much from yourself)
7. You often feel resentment (when you expect too much from other people)
8. You have negative core beliefs (e.g. I have to be skinny to find a boyfriend)
9. You feel overly disappointed, frustrated, heartbroken, or depressed when things don't go your way (or how you expected them to go)
10. Your relationships are suffering because of poor communication or fighting

Whenever you want to change something, you need to first acknowledge that it exists and it is a problem.

So the first step in how to let go of your expectations is to realize that you have expectations and then identify what they are.

1. What are your expectations of yourself?
2. What do you consciously and unconsciously expect of others?
3. What are your expectations regarding events in your life, your future dreams, and the world in general?

It's a good idea to journal about your expectations so you can become consciously aware of the expectations you have.

You can't always take time and write about your expectations, so eventually, you want to move toward being mindful about having expectations.

Next, you need to put each expectation into perspective. Is this expectation something you have control over? If it is, turn it into a goal so you can adjust your thoughts and actions according to how reality unfolds. If the expectation isn't something you can control, move to the next step.

Once you know you have expectations and you know what they are, you can work on changing your mindset. You want to think about things differently.

When you have an expectation about something and things don't turn out the way you wanted (or expected) them to, it's easy to fall into a negative mindset. A bad hour easily turns into a bad day, which can quickly become a bad week.

This kind of mindset where you are disappointed, angry, and hurt because things didn't go your way doesn't serve a purpose. Instead, you need to take control and think about yourself, events, others, and life differently.

Try to think positively about the situation – see a setback with optimism and ask what the lesson was. Also, focus on what you are doing and the good and not what you may be missing out on.

Choosing to find the positive in any situation helps you practice gratitude and appreciation – identify and focus on what you have. It's a space to enjoy the present.

Part of changing your mindset is cultivating your inner voice or dialog.

Are you kind in the way you speak to yourself?

Do your thoughts reflect who you are and who you want to be?

Or do they focus on who you should be (which is an expectation)?

What you see reflects your thinking, and your thinking but reflects the choice of what you want to see.

1. Your expectations can determine your experience.
2. What you pay attention to changes your perception.

You can change both expectations and attention to increase happiness and well-being.

Expectation

We live in a way that our life operates much like an echo chamber. Have you ever seen the Kevin Hart "Cash Back" commercial?

He said: Hellooooo Cash Back and the echo chamber say Hellooooo Kevin Hart. That is what wealth creation can be like in your life.

What goes out comes back to you over and over again. If you think about how you look and feel when you are in a good mood—and when you are in a sour mood—you'll have a sense of how this works.

It begins with what you put out. If we are joyous, hopeful, or grateful, we see joy, hope, and gratitude. If we are uncertain, anxious, and hopeless, we see through goggles that present a world of despair.

Your expectation of what is to come does the job of interpreting life for you. Your reaction then loops into a confirmation bias. This means you will experience life as expected. Your beliefs and expectations about what is to come get confirmed by your experience.

There is a loop. It is bidirectional—meaning that your interpretation creates the experience confirming the interpretation. It's almost as if you are responding to a form of self-hypnosis.

Good or not-so-good, you put what you believe you are experiencing into your life, and you will confirm it. Just start saving that $19.76 a day, a week or bi-weekly and experience the transformation.

There were these studies that I was reading where the subjects were hypnotized and told they would be touched very briefly with a lump of hot coal. The researchers then touched the subjects with an ice cube. Immediately the participants formed a blister where they were touched.

Anticipating something bad would happen put them in a state where they felt they had to protect themselves—even when there was no need to—and there were consequences.

Your power of expectation also works protectively. Under hypnosis, subjects allergic to various substances were found able to inhibit a reaction when told they would not be affected.

In those studies, the stimulus was perceived differently based on what was expected. An ice cube can cause a blister if it is expected to burn you, and an allergic reaction can be neutralized if the allergen is perceived as harmless.

How you expect something will deeply influence how you respond. This is particularly true when you think about your future wealth creation and legacy. What you expect is what you detect—what you believe, you perceive.

I've seen this demonstration many different ways, look at this duck drawing and notice how long his beak is.

Now, look at the same image, and what if I asked you to look at the rabbit's nose and how long his ears are? If you let your eyes drift over to the right, the "duck" becomes a "rabbit," and then shifting back, the image becomes a duck.

The image, the stimulus, and the input didn't change—but how you looked at it did. What you expected is what was detected.

You saw two completely different animals because of expectations—and what you directed your attention to. If I had told you to look at the rabbit first—that is what you would have initially seen. Expectations create the experience.

What do you see?

What you perceive with the duck/rabbit depends on where you focus. Two different animals facing opposite directions.

Your experience changes depending on what you are centered on. If you want to see a duck—keep staring at the beak. If you like rabbits, look the other way. You can choose how it will be seen.

Let me say it this way. If you want to see and experience wealth creation and generational wealth you have to change what you are focusing on if it is not the results you want.

You can also choose how you think about your future. In fact, how you think about yourself in the future increases positive feelings in the moment and positive future expectations. Imagining a positive future self creates an expectation that results in greater optimism, higher life satisfaction, less depression, greater happiness, and well-being.

Your thoughts are not happening to you—they are happening for you. Learning how to harness the power of positive expectations allows you to use your thoughts like a powerful flashlight to find the best path forward.

Here is a way to begin cultivating positive expectations. It starts with knowing there is an alternative way of experiencing your financial situation.

Changing How You Think

1. When you are in a negative mood and cannot see or take in positive experiences, challenge your perception by using the sentence, "There is another way to look at this."

This declarative sentence allows your thoughts to be challenged by opening up the possibility of an alternate way of seeing the situation. It is like reminding you that there may be another way of seeing this image than as a duck.

2. Make a list of these other (more positive) ways of seeing the situation as viable and acknowledge them.

3. Finally, deliberately take time to review the items on your list and allow yourself to feel gratitude for these more positive ways of viewing the situation.

Chapter Four

Reimagine

As in the previous chapters, I want to elaborate on how beneficial your strategy to focus on wealth creation is to you. Nothing else, this is about you reimagining yourself from your past experiences by considering how you were affected by or have seen wealth around as you reflect back.

Why is reflection important for your wealth creation?

Reflection — is a process where you learn to review or even describe how your financial life has been in the past and how it changed, and how it very well may relate to your future learning experiences with money.

Please understand that it is a skill that often goes undervalued in our life experiences and is packed with content for learning. I reflect back to a time in my life that I was introduced to "Soft Butter", it made an impression on my life.

As a kid I was always in trouble, growing up poor I was limited in my experience and knowledge regarding basic foods.

We received welfare food in the seventies, powdered eggs, powdered milk, cheese (pound for pound the best cheese ever) and butter. Oh, I cannot leave out the yellow grain grits, not buttered or cheese grits – YELLOW.

So this doctor decided to pour into me by allowing me to work with him on Saturdays at his home. Every Saturday morning I would outside work in his yard, I would occasionally peep in the house and watch them eat breakfast.

He had two daughters and they would always catch me peeping in the window as they ate. On one of those mornings he came out and invited me in for breakfast. What a life experience it was for me. They had fresh sliced baked bread and took a knife and spread something over it, I first thought it was some kind of jelly, but it wasn't, it was soft butter.

Oh my goodness, I can recall the sweetness of the favor at this moment, the impact was there at the time but not truly realized until I reflected back to that moment. I do recall going back home and sharing that experience with my family only to be laughed at.

Then I begin to recognize the frequency of this commercial that played and again listen to my family laugh at me. That commercial was “Parkay – Butter – Parkaaay” I believe Deacon Jones was in one of them, it was clearly a reflection that gave me a vision outside of poverty.

However, reflection is important, it helps to make sense of and grow from a learning experience, and it should be a practice that if you are focusing on wealth creation that you develop. Let me be clear, reflecting is an important practice across many various disciplines including job performance, nursing, business, the sciences and more.

Therefore you should be exposing yourself to continuous reflective thinking practices so that you can become "creator" and not "consumers" of wealth.

Listen, I believe there will be a phenomenon in which new and unfamiliar thinking approaches through the application, remixing or integration of previous knowledge, skills, strategies, and dispositions that will create habits of the mind that leads to the success of wealth creation..

Your goal with reflection is putting many perspectives into play with each other in order to produce your insight. Simply looking forward to goals you might attain, as well as a casting backward to see where you have been.

When you reflect/reimagine, you thus project and review, often putting the projections and the reviews in sync with each other, and working to discover what you know, what you have learned, and what you might understand.

I know that just talking about reflection can be a set-up to failure, another sound good feel good moment that leads to only a 72 hour knowledge high.

After all your reflection is what you see in the mirror. But there are other things that bounce back at you are also reflections — light waves, sound waves, even your thoughts.

I went to the dictionary on the word. "Reflection comes from the Latin reflectere, made up of the prefix re-, "back," and flectere, "to bend." So it's bending something back: your reflection in the mirror is the light waves that bounce your image back at you."

This hold thing on wealth creation is about your readiness, your willingness and your focus, your past problems and hinderers. But at the same time, you probably should do some serious thinking about what readiness actually means to you.

This places more importance on the manner in which the thinking should be done. It implies that although you might have thought about it before/were planning on thinking about it, you should treat it in a serious (rather than insignificant) way.

All that being said, the difference in using either in your sentence is pretty minor. It's just a matter of phrasing and/or emphatic context.

I do not know about you, but I like many of clients that were willing to share that they had a lot of sleepless nights. Nights, when they were so worried about something that had happened in their past that has created hardship that is now dictating their future. We've all been there at some point. You're not alone.

I'm talking about those times when you just can't shake the past. Whether it's something small, like making a terrible first impression, or saying something you wish you hadn't, to something big, like having to shut down your ability for wealth creation. Harping on negative experiences is painful and, when you hold on to that pain, you can't move on to something more positive in your life.

That's why it's important that you let it go and leave the past behind and learn from the past but don't dwell there. If by chance there are areas to reimagine and find your greatness this is it.

So, let's deal with those negative experiences by reimagining something new and different. Today I am in my sixties, that painful past had set me up to be viewed as a loser, most likely to end up dead or in jail by age 21. But during the age year of 19, I begin to reimagine myself, knowing what I was and desiring thing so much more.(Soft Butter)

Your negative experiences that you had can actually be used for learning and future experiences -- no matter how painful they are. Take some time to reflect/reimagine on the experience and look at ways it can actually benefit you down the road. Try learning from your experiences by reflecting on these few simple questions:

What really happened to me or with me? Answer only by confronting the facts.

____

____

____

What emotions do I feel? I personally like to write them down.

____

____

____

Reimagine

How can I use this to empower myself and my feelings?

____

____

____

After answering these questions, it's time to move on. While reflecting on the past for a little bit of time is acceptable, dwelling on it will only keep those negative thoughts and feelings around.

Moving on from your DNA can be difficult. Reflecting can trap you if you don't move on, I think about clients who are still angry and hurt from their past. They cannot seem to let this go, the anger and resentment will not allow them to reimagine life.

So, whatever you have to do, don't hesitate to get the pain you're feeling off your chest. Whether it's talking to the individual who has harmed you (or who you harmed), venting to a friend or writing it down, expressing your feelings can assist you in sorting out what, if anything, needs to be done to move on.

I talked about this in "Wealth Creation The Mindset" and tried to warn you that holding onto your feelings leads to anxiety, depression, headache and high blood pressure.

When it's time to express your feelings, make sure to use "I" messages. Real simple, I am responsible. I am the cause, I need to fit this. Always try to describe the degree of your emotions, and share them with someone who will listen and not pass judgment. This will help you express any grief you're going through.

Reflection should not have you playing the role of the victim. It is very easy and sometimes feels pretty good, especially compared with accepting the truth. The problem is, blaming others prevents you from going forward. Most often, pointing fingers is just complaining.

I said this earlier, this is about you. Reflecting can cause you to want to shift the responsibility on others. What is sad about this is blaming others gives power to someone else and makes you small.

Please remember when you blame, you automatically enter the negative zone. You loathe someone else or some external factor because you were not able to mold life into your own favor.

I stayed broke blaming others, when I was homeless it was not my fault. Have you ever heard of the five chapters of life?

CHAPTER 1

I walk down the street.
There's a deep hole in the sidewalk.
And I fall in.
I am lost. I am helpless. It isn't my fault.
It takes forever to find a way out.

CHAPTER 2

I walk down the same street.
There is a deep hole in the sidewalk.
I pretend I don't see it. I fall in again.
I can't believe I am in the same place.
But it isn't my fault.
It takes a long time to get out.

CHAPTER 3

I walk down the same street and there is a deep hole in the sidewalk.
I see it there, and still I fall in.
It's a habit.
But my eyes are open and I know where I am.
It is my fault and I get out immediately.

CHAPTER 4

I walk down the same street.
There is a deep hole in the sidewalk.
I walk around it.

CHAPTER 5

I walk down a different street.
By Portia Nelson

Your ability to create wealth and create generational wealth for your family really is about you going a different direction.

What I have discovered in all of my years in this financial space is that we actually see the destination. You see elements of wealth all around you daily, you feel lost and helpless and it's not your fault.

Yet you stay in the same place, not able to move on and unable to save money or invest. Just stuck right there where you are not willing to move. Where is your readiness? You must begin focusing on right now, reimagine and renew your dreams and your readiness.

Today, begin focusing on this moment, begin focusing on the present. One of the most effective ways to let go of the past is to embrace your present. Instead of reliving the past and getting consumed with negativity, keep yourself active and enjoy the current moment.

Whatever it takes, learn a new skill. Meditate. Exercise. Have dinner with a friend. Make a new friend. Take a financial class. Read a book. Whatever it is, just live in the moment - even if it's just sitting at thinking of anything that causes you to grow.

Oftentimes I enjoy watching the sunset or watching the clouds roll by. In the past I personally "focus" by building my business and the future. It motivates me and helps give me something to devote my life towards. Wealth Creation

Living in the moment, is not this thing called “living my best life”. Living in the moment is not a “bucket list”. Living in the moment is not “a boss life”.

Living in the moment, is also called mindfulness, "involves being with your thoughts as they are, neither grasping at them nor pushing them away." I bet you didn't know that mindful people are happier, more exuberant, more empathetic, and more secure.

You can achieve a more mindful state, always be aware of what you are thinking and feeling, reduce self-consciousness, seek out new experiences with finance and accept and see your negative feelings and situations as merely being a part of life and reimagine them.

The next chapter is going to be about being intentional with your actions, your thoughts, your feelings and your abilities. As you reflect and reimagine, also allow yourself to take some time away so that you can clear your head.

You don't have to go backpacking or camping. Just remove yourself from the situation by distancing yourself from the people, places and things that remind you of the past. Practicing ways to disconnect for a while will give you the chance to experience something positive. When you return, you'll have a new perspective on the past.

Your life is as strong as the circle around. I am not sure where this quote came from, but I know it to be very powerful. “If nine (9) of your closest friends are broke, guess who number ten (10) will be.” Reflect and think about the people around you.

You may not feel comfortable taking inventory of the people around you. Who is negative and always bringing you down? Who are the people associated with the past that you're trying to move away from?

Who is it that has used you as an ATM? You may need to move away from these individuals to find more positive people who will empower you.

There are more than enough ways to meet new people, such as attending local meetups and conferences. Don't be shy. Get yourself out there and find a new group of friends and acquaintances who can help you move forward.

There are financial and investment events everywhere today, just be mindful of who you are getting close to as if you were about to give them your money.

Another important aspect of your reimagining will call for you to forgive any of those people who wronged you – and this is including yourself. When you have been hurt by someone, the last thing that you may want to do is forgive them.

Forgiving others is essential for spiritual growth. Steps to help you forgive someone, can be like embracing the past while moving on, making a new agreement with yourself, not going to sleep angry and being kind and generous.

While you're at it, forgive yourself. No one is perfect and we all make mistakes. Instead of kicking yourself for your past mistakes, cut yourself some slack and focus on the lessons that you've learned. Once you're not carrying that anger and resentment, you'll be able to move on. Reimagine

Then you are able to get to the fun part, make new memories. Finally, start making new, positive memories to replace those negative memories from the past. Spend your time with the people who make you happy, the things that bring you joy and in the places that bring you peace. Making new memories is better than being stuck in the past.

New Bank
New Brokerage Account
New Investments
New Portfolio
New Saving
New Incomes
New.

In fact, having too many old memories makes it more difficult to make new memories. So, out with the old and in with the new focus.

Chapter Five

Intentional

Something that is sticking with me from the last chapter that I believe is really going to be life changing for you and your wealth creation journey. Remember the statement "seriously thinking or thinking seriously", if not go back and read it again.

Because now you are entering another zone regarding your focus which becomes "intentionally intentional".

The fact that you are reading this series on wealth creation means you want to change something about yourself, you want to even transform your life into something completely different.

You can do it when you act with purposeful intention. Attempting to change without being intentional during the process will not meet with much success.

I remember reading the book "The Slight Edge", one of the simple things I learned at first was that the pattern of my life already had commitment and deliberate actions. Just in a destructive way. Every day I was doing the same things that added no value to my future dreams (I am not sure I even had dreams).

I was intentional with what I was doing. Likewise, so are you, every time when you say you will act with intention, what actually does that mean? It seems that on the surface of things you like I act with intention every day, even for the same activities day in and day out.

You are already mastering being intentional. Think about it, you intend to set the alarm to get up and go to work. So you do. You intend to pick the kids up from school. So you do. You intend to watch this TV program or read that magazine. So you do.

The crazy thing about you is that you intend on saving money. So you don't. You intend to open a brokerage account. So you don't. You intend to invest. So you don't.

There are also many other things that you intend to do that you never do. You intend to have the neighbors over for dinner. But, you never do. You intend to help out at the local charity.

But, you never do. You intend to leave that life-force sucking job that you hate and move on to something better. But, you never do. You intend to create wealth. But…

If you intend to change but do not, then it would seem that you are actually intending not to change. Remember, intention is just a mental thought process.

What's the difference between the two intentions – to intend to do something and do it on the one hand and to intend to do something and not do it on the other? Is there a difference? Yes, I believe there is.

I believe that what people actually and precisely mean to "acting with intention" or being "intentional" is that they are proclaiming to be intentionally intentional. Intentional living is something that has caught on in the past few years.

People want to do work that has meaning and live out a purpose. Being a better money manager and wealth creator can be looked at the same way.

Wealth is not something that you just hope into, it is more about how you handle money. I must admit that some days are just on the impulse of people. There is no rhythm or rhyme to the course of the day as they move through it.

Being intentional with your money not only helps prevent lifestyle inflation, but it is also a key component of creating wealth within a budget that works for you. Let me define intentional as simply being "done on purpose." In other words, when you do something intentionally you mean to do it.

Likewise intentional spending, saving and investing is when you spend, save and invest money with purpose. It's when you're deliberate and mindful in your decisions. Intentional spending, saving and investing, is the opposite of impulse spending, saving and investing.

I could only hope that by now, you've probably begun to understand the benefits of being intentional with your money.

But what does intentional spending, saving and investing really mean? If you're like most people, you tend to put off thinking about financial matters until an emergency pops up or something needs to be purchased.

With inflation rates currently skyrocketing through the roof all over the world, now's a good time to stop waiting for an emergency and start being more intentionally intentional about where your money is going.

So many people believe that it's always more, more money and their most important job is to figure out how to get paid more. I completely disagree with that idea.

Let's look beyond the obviousness of income to say your most important job is to figure out how to live on less than what you earn. It sounds so intimidating, but it's feasible if you look at things holistically and start with purpose.

A few questions here:

- How often do you buy things on impulse or when you didn't mean to?
- How often are you tempted and overcome by the amount of deliciousness at the checkout in the grocery store?
- How many times have you grabbed that candy bar, even though you don't mean to?
- Did you know that the same impulse buying scenario can be intentional as well though?

Some of you will make a conscious choice to set aside a certain amount each month specifically for impulse buys and you don't go over that amount, then you are managing your money intentionally. But this money is not for wealth creation.

However, being intentional is all about making the decisions and sticking to them. You made a choice to set aside money that you can spend impulsively. You made the choice. Make the choice of saving and investing.

Your intentional spending, saving and investing means you are being aware of where your money is going, and putting it towards things of real value.

Do some soul searching to find out exactly what you value.

For example, I value giving and generosity as well as families. I intentionally put my money toward a ministry that specializes in ministering to families. I have no issue giving to this ministry because it aligns with my values.

Some of you may value eating clean or sustainably. This usually costs more money than the cheap grocery store items that are filled with chemicals so it's important to make a conscious decision to put your money toward it. Right? The same is true to wealth creation.

You may have a passion for caring for the environment and not being overly wasteful. This may prevent you from drinking single-serve pod coffee and instead opt for more expensive fair trade coffee.

No matter what your values are, be confident in them. They are a part of who you are and should be reflected in what you do with your money.

It can be hard to figure out your values, I value being able to teach people how to manage their money and create wealth, but I didn't develop that passion by being passive about it. It took some work determining what I value.

No one can or should decide what you value for you. However, I hope that I can help you get there. Now go to one of your favorite places, a place where you can relax and clear your mind without being interrupted. Are you there yet? If not, stop reading until you actually do this.

Now, try and clear your mind of everything else that is going on around you. Lastly, relax. There will be no right or wrong answers when it comes to your values. Just own them.

Think back on your life, identify the following five things:

When were you most satisfied?
When were you the happiest?
What activities make you the proudest?
What do you really desire for you?
What commitments have you made that you value?

The way I manage my money aligns with my values so I don't mind spending and/or saving money in order to allow myself more time to do those things. It's intentionally intentional on my part.

If you are going to be intentional about living below your means or your income, let's be clear about something. Living below your income does not mean that you devalue the quality of your life in any form.

Now you must become intentional about your goals. You see when you know your values it takes care of the present. Knowing your goals will help take care of your future.

Your goals should align with your values as well, but you have to know what your goals are in order to create wealth intentionally.

To add to this, intentional spending, saving and investing is a mindful and purposeful way of wealth creation. It means being aware of your spending habits and making choices that align not only with your personal means, but with your values and goals.

For example, if you value health and fitness, you might choose to spend more on healthy food and activities which support your health.

Or, if travel and happenings are important to you, you might choose to spend more on experiences that will create lasting memories.

There are different takes on how to be intentional with your money. One is to create a process that reflects your values and goals. This can help you see where your money is going so you can make better choices. First though, you need to know what your intention is, and what you truly value.

Intention is the determination to act a certain way. With devoted deliberation and purpose. To manage your spending, saving and invest intentionally, focus on your goal.

It might be something very specific, such as wanting to save up for a new home, or to simply build wealth for early retirement.

In either case, take a step back and think about your particular situation and what you're unhappy with. Like what's important to you, what you truly value, and what you are not willing to sacrifice.

Once you really understand why you want to change your spending habits and what's important to you, you'll have the focus it takes for intentional wealth creation.

You must ask yourself a question; Why are goals so important?

With no goal, there is no way to tell where the end is. Setting a goal gives you something to target.

Another important part of having goals is that it gives you better insight on if you are doing the right things to get there. If you have clear goals, you can measure the things you're doing and tell if you're getting closer or farther from your goal.

As you focus you learn how important it is to set your goals. Think about what you want to improve in your life.

For instance, I want to continue to improve as a writer so I have a goal to write a certain word count a day. This gives me practice writing every single day. In addition, I take online courses to improve as well.

I like for you to set goals for different timelines in your life. I prefer that you use a different approach than small goals first. Put generational wealth as your very first goal as you walk your way back to daily goals.

Let's get started:

Five-year Goal(s)

____

____

____

Yearly Goal(s)

____

____

____

Monthly Goal(s)

____

____

____

Weekly Goal(s)

____

____

____

Daily Goal(s)

____

____

____

What seems to work for most of my clients is setting more goals the longer the time frame. For example, you set only one goal to achieve in a day or a week—one thing to focus on—but you may have a couple of goals for monthly and quite a few five-year goals.

The order you list them in is no accident as well. Usually, what you determine your five or one-year goal to be will inform your daily, weekly, and monthly goals.

Set daily, weekly, and monthly goals that will help you get to your one-year or five-year goals. Set each goal intentionally!

Now that you know what your values and what your goals are, you can really be intentional with your money.

This is where all of that other great advice comes into play. Here are some tools and methods you can use to help you manage your money with intention:

1. Track your spending
2. Budget to align with your values
3. Set up automatic savings

4. Set up automatic investing
5. Don't spend your money on things that won't bring you value

These are all great methods to help you manage your money with intention.

This is precisely what I mean about intentionality. It aligned perfectly with my values. The trip helped strengthen my relationship with my kids and with my wife, gave us a chance to get away from home and let us get away from our jobs for an extra day.

Knowing your goals and your values are what really sets apart your finances from someone else's. You can't really be intentional with your money if you don't know those two areas.

You can track your spending and budget all you want, but those are really just methods to help you spend intentionally.

Intentional wealth creation may sound lofty, complicated, or just plain confusing. But it's a way of life that you can build with some reflection and small shifts. Intentional wealth creation is all about focusing on your purpose and core values. You've likely heard about living an intentional life.

It seems like intentional wealth creation is everywhere these days. But what does it really mean to be intentional? What does it look like to do things with intention? And perhaps most important, intentional wealth creation is available to everyone.

It is — anyone can lead an intentional, purpose-filled life. The key is to identify what that personally means for you — and make small but still significant shifts and conscious choices to build it. Intentional wealth creation means building your life around your core beliefs and values.

What might intentional living look like day-to-day? I hope you think it looks like not acting on impulse or merely existing.

Rather, it's about commanding your days. Trust me when I tell you intentional living can lower your stress. One reason is that you stop weighing the pros and cons of every decision, which causes you so much anxiety.

Man oh Man, if you could just understand how your focus power is fueled by you being intentional. Being intentional give you power like:

- Creates a sense of agency in your lives
- Gives you access to your own power
- Supports you in feeling more present, in tune, and capable

An intentional life brings meaning, profound satisfaction, and fulfillment because you're living in a way that's true to who you are. While intentional living is powerful, it's not always joyful, peaceful, or easy. Sometimes, it can be challenging and even awkward — especially in the beginning.

What you might realize at some point is that the values and traditions you learned from your family, culture, or society no longer resonate with you — and that "can be tough to navigate."

It is a fact that as you get closer to the core of what matters to you, you could lean away from activities and relationships that numbed or distracted you and toward new, healthier patterns. And at first, that can feel foreign and uncomfortable.

But remember that many worthwhile things can be tough sometimes. The key is to keep going, reminding yourself that you're building a life that aligns with your deepest principles. A life being intentionally intentional.

I have found that naming your values is the foundation of living an intentional life. Answering these questions can help you get some clarity on what's vital to you:

- From morning to night, what does an ideal day look like for you?
- Why are these things so important?
- What are the activities that bring you fulfillment? Meaning? Contentment?
- What do these activities have in common?
- What do you wish you had more of? Or Less of?
- What upsets you?
- What inspires you?

Try setting a morning intention, your intention may be a few words or a sentence. It may serve as a reminder of how you'd like to behave and the choices you'd like to make that day.

You can make your intention-setting part of a larger morning ritual that includes a brief meditation practice and giving thanks. Or, you can simply close your eyes, put your hands over your heart, and recite your intention before getting out of bed.

Here's the thing about living an intentional life: You don't need to overhaul your entire life, or start from scratch. You can infuse intentionality into activities you're already doing and actions you're already taking,

I am probably sounding like a broken record by now. Intentional living comes from living out your values. This means taking actions and making decisions that are important to you and true to who you are.

Intentional living also becomes an everyday practice that we might fall in and out of, knowing we can always start again at any moment.

An intentional life brings joy and lowers stress. But sometimes, particularly when you're making some changes, it can and will be difficult — especially if your current intentions don't line up with what you've learned in your early life.

Remind yourself that it's totally natural to feel a range of emotions while on an intentional living path. After all, you're a human being doing the best you can.

I want you to know being intentional is about bringing a commitment, focus, and attention to something important to you. If you want to be intentional every day you need to get clear upfront about what you want to achieve and then take action on achieving it.

You being intentional is a capability you can grow every day and will change your life. To move your life forward and make progress every day, being intentional about what is important to you and then taking action on those things will be two guiding qualities.

You being intentional helps you become more present and achieve bigger and better goals in your wealth creation life. When you are intentional, you bring a clear purpose, structure, and positive mindset to your day.

Remember, you being intentional means having the ability to see specific results in the future that, if you achieve them, will make things bigger and better for yourself, your family, and wealth creation.

You must have an intentional focus in your way of thinking about your wealth and life that's committed, purposeful, and deliberate. When you are intentional, you choose to make decisions and take action on what's important to you. Being intentional means getting clear upfront about what you want to achieve.

You intentionally set an intention to achieve a specific outcome or result in the future that is important to you. This could be a goal you want to achieve or something you want to have in your life. It is not always about money.

You then move forward with intention every day towards achieving the result or outcome you want. Being intentional increases your focus on what's most important to you.

It is important to be more intentional with your time.

I want you to grow to a point that you have a clear purpose and are intentional about taking action on the thoughts and feelings that are most important to you.

When you have an intentional focus, you choose to live and create a life that has a clear purpose and is meaningful and exciting to you.

Choosing to take action on the things that are important to you allows you to live with intention where you consciously choose to create the life you want, rather than having other people dictate your feelings and actions.

Being an intentional person means everything you do is done with a clear purpose and focus. When you become intentional, you focus your time and energy on your strengths, and the good things in your life, and don't let fear hold you back.

Intentional people are action-oriented and have an unshakeable determination and strong mindset to accomplish what they've set out to achieve. To become more intentional, it's important to be self-aware, say no more than you say yes, and practice gratitude.

With intentionality, you appreciate more and practice gratitude for the things that matter most in your life. When you are intentional, you set better boundaries around your time and the areas of your life that are important. When you are intentional, you focus on abundance.

I need you to be deliberate with your day, every day. MAN, I DON'T KNOW HOW TO DRILL THIS IN. When you are intentional with your time, energy, and focus each day, you are far more likely to achieve the result you want.

Being intentional with your time ensures you have a clear structure for your day and allows you to establish daily routines that support your goals.

When you have greater direction and purpose, you know exactly where to invest your time, attention and money. Your time is aligned with your bigger purpose which increases your opportunity for wealth creation.

Intentional

Without an intentional focus for your day, you can feel stuck and waste time on non-important activities. Without intention, you can take on too much and get easily distracted.

To be more deliberate with your day, identify the three important activities that will help you achieve the outcome you want.

This will ensure you feel proud about what you've achieved, which boosts confidence and self-esteem.

1.
2.
3.

Having an intentional commitment to what you want aligns your actions with your goals and ensures you focus your time on your biggest priorities. Be clear on your vision and act with purpose with the goals you set.

You must be clear on the result you want. You can increase your intentionality by getting clarity on the measurable results you want to achieve in the future. When you are clear on the results you want and understand the importance of achieving those results, you will be more intentional.

I plan to dive into vision a little late. But, aligning your vision with measurable goals ensures you are motivated and focused to take action.

To be more intentional, get clear upfront about the outcome you want through powerful goal setting. Picture yourself having achieved your goal to understand the importance of your goals.

When you have an emotional investment in your bigger purpose and goals, you are intentional about taking action. Seeing what your life looks like once you've achieved your goals increases your confidence and ensures you feel motivated every day.

I was recently working with a client who was ready for change. After going over her numbers and her goals we created a model for under eight years that allows her to purchase and pay off a $350,000.00 house and a $50,000.00 car while saving and investing over $300,000.00.

Initially, she could not picture how she could possibly do this target with having to take on other jobs. But as we go her number map the plan, she now sees what it looks like for her future. She even began to recognize some other possibilities that she could accomplish.

Act on your greater purpose by setting measurable goals that you will focus on. Everything that you do from this point is about you being purposeful with your time.

Hear me when I say being intentional is all about being purposeful with your time to help you achieve your most important goals. When you are intentional with your time, you have a clear structure for your day and establish positive daily habits and routines.

It is only a secret to unintentional people because intentional people understand the importance of their time and look to achieve their goals in the simplest, easiest, and fastest way possible.

Intentional

To be intentional with your time, it's important to understand that certain priorities, relationships, and collaborations will help you achieve the results you want.

To be purposeful with your time, set boundaries around your time, set aside time for self-care, and plan around your energy levels. Starting and ending each day with gratitude will help you protect your time and ensure you end each day feeling proud of what you've achieved.

And another thing, you must be considered with your focus. Intentionality increases your focus on the things and people that are most important to you including wealth creation. Intentionality helps you understand the importance and purpose of your bigger vision and directs your mind and actions to help you achieve it.

An intentional focus gives you greater clarity around what you want and takes the guesswork out of where to invest your time, focus and money. Being intentional with your focus ensures you prioritize effectively and have a clear structure for your day based on your bigger purpose.

Having this focus on your vision, and knowing the action steps you need to take, gives you the confidence to focus your attention on what matters most to you.

Wealth creation will not just happen in your life because you made a few investments or you avoided some taxes, it is bigger than that.

I know that you have heard it before, intentional goals allow you to align your purpose and vision with an action plan to achieve your goals.

When you are intentional about your goals, you identify the result you want to achieve upfront which gives you more direction and focus.

Setting goals gives you a plan and path to work towards every day and ensures you start your day with focus and purpose. Goals give you the motivation and focus to achieve your priorities in life.

When your goals are clear, you know why you want to achieve your goals and when you want to achieve your goals. This clarity gives you the confidence to structure your time. It also helps you invest your time, energy and money in your biggest priorities (wealth creation).

Intentionality increases the value of your most important relationships and brings deeper meaning to them. When you appreciate your most important relationships, you experience greater gratitude, abundance and self-awareness.

It helps you understand the purpose and importance of every relationship you have. When you take the time to understand why a relationship is important, you feel happier and more joyful.

When you express gratitude to someone, their value in your life grows. Identifying what you want from a relationship ensures you are clear about the best result you want from that relationship.

When you focus on being intentional every day you feel clearer, more capable, and more confident. To be intentional, get clear upfront on exactly what you want to achieve, understand its importance, and take focused action every day towards achieving the things that matter most.

Being purposeful and deliberate builds a positive mindset, helps you become more present in the moment, and gives your life greater clarity and meaning.

Chapter Six

Purpose

I realize that I talked about goals and goal setting in previous writing. Each time I have connected it with a different stage of your growth. The principle will never change, the application can and will vary. A part of being purposeful is having goals and being motivated by your values. It's important for you to understand this as you build your focus.

When you are setting goals in your home and life it can be challenging, especially when the goals that need to be set impact others – it's significant. Often, these goals are created and developed with good intentions, but not enough action happens around them after the initial frenzy.

You must have proper alignment, goals can give a sense of purpose. Setting goals gives a reason for doing what you are doing and clears the path for you to find out how to achieve it.

The setting goals can be of multiple types – from home to family to wealth creation. In all its forms, goal setting involves achieving a target within a set time frame. Yes these goals can be 'learning a new skill' or 'improving an old skill,' and for wealth creation – they can be as lofty as changing the way the wealth is accumulated.

The focus is achieving set goals, this process is the simplest and the best way to identify when a project is complete. Having goals that clearly define success allows you to focus on the result that must be achieved by the deadline.

Meeting goals can help you feel more fulfilled, and it can also bolster overall satisfaction and accomplishment. As tracking the progress of the plan can help family members and those around you understand the contribution of their efforts better in the larger scheme of things, they'll likely feel more valued and appreciated. This increase in loyalty means better relationship all around

Okay, I have been waiting to get right here. (This Part) you have to be smart about it. I know you have heard and seen this before, this time make it matter. Here are the five keys to goal setting?

The main criteria of goals are that you should be **S.M.A.R.T.** – and the acronym stands for specific, measurable, achievable, relevant, and time-bound. These five keys ensure the goals set are meaningful and focus on the development of the entire household.

Specific

Any goal that calls for improvement must explicitly mention a specific end. Be it increasing savings, buying a home, or investing more in stocks – making the goal as specific as possible ensures better planning and execution of the vision.

Measurable

Sometimes, even specific goals with definitive ends may not be measurable. If that is the case, then you should go back to the drawing board and find another specific goal. A way to measure progress gives you an idea if you are on the right track and allows you to intervene if results are way off the expected mark.

Achievable

Keeping goals grounded in reality and just out of reach keep you on your toes – and helps you improve your skills to achieve.

Relevant

Saving $19.76 a day or a week for a year is a Specific, measurable, and achievable goal – and it is relevant? Setting goals and talking about it will not lead to progress. In the current financial world, you have to constantly look for new ways to invest – and targeting relevant goals is the best way to stay on top of the game.

Time-bound

Lofty goals without specific end times are just wishes, nothing else. Without a timeline, you will likely push off achieving the goals.

The message here is goals that end up being effective start as intentional ones. How you define goals and matching milestones greatly assists you in identifying potential roadblocks, capitalizing on the momentum, and achieving the results you desire. You should aim to do more than just hope and dream and think about what's ahead.

I know better than anyone, when it comes to wealth creation, everyone's situation is unique. No one has the same bills, rent, debts, lifestyle or income. When you're ready to take control of your financial lifestyle, you need a plan that will answer your specific goals, not your neighbor's.

Your financial goals are a target to aim for when managing your money. It does involve saving, spending, earning, or even investing. Wealth creation requires that you have a clear picture of what you're aiming for, working towards your target may not be easy. I just talked about how your goals should be measurable, specific, and time-oriented.

Let me get this out of the way. Having an emergency fund or saving for emergencies is one of the only goals that is a necessity. It should be the first one you should set, regardless of your situation. Life is unpredictable, and it's important to be prepared.

But please realize this is not wealth creation, it's a part of the foundation. When something unexpected and expensive occurs, emergency funds are there to keep you from suffering the financial blow.

Paying off debts is not a financial goal. It is your obligation and no one feels comfortable knowing that they owe large sums of money. And because the amount you owe is already a specific number, paying off debt can easily be eliminated.

Making every monthly payment on time is not enough, your best way to make real progress is to stop borrowing. Adding to your debt will only push you away from your ability to create wealth, so it's important to stay strong and diligent.

Buying a home is a financial goal right now. Whether you're saving for a down payment or working to pay off a mortgage, homeownership is one of the largest financial targets to aim for. Your life purpose consists of the central motivating aims of your life—the reasons you get up in the morning.

Purpose can guide life decisions, influence behavior, shape goals, offer a sense of direction, and create meaning. For some people, purpose is connected to vocation—meaningful, satisfying work.

For others, their purpose lies in their responsibilities to their family or friends. Others seek meaning through spirituality or religious beliefs. Some people may find their purpose clearly expressed in all these aspects of life.

Purpose will be unique for everyone; what you identify as your path may be different from others. What's more, your purpose can actually shift and change throughout life in response to the evolving priorities and fluctuations of your own experiences.

Some people feel hesitant about pursuing their life purpose because they worry that it sounds like a self-serving or selfish quest. However, the true purpose is about recognizing your own gifts and using them to contribute to the world—whether those gifts are playing beautiful music for others to enjoy, helping friends solve problems, or simply bringing more joy into the lives of those around you.

Now, I will start out by asking you a few questions. Who are you? Seriously, who are you? Who are you as the provider? Who are you as a visionary? We are still in the rhyme of Wealth Creation The Focus, we must talk about purpose and purpose in a different way.

For most people it is in our nature to strive, to want, and move in a direction of something we desire and deem valuable. I honestly believe that your nature is to become a link or the first link to generational wealth and legacy transfer. This is your reason for purpose, to focus on something bigger than yourself.

Purpose is connection to a goal bigger than yourself; self-organizing aims that guides you and imbues even the simplest actions with relevance and meaning. It goes beyond a simple goal or objective because it's focused on the long-term and on a deeper meaning. It is all about finding and engaging your life purpose.

If I can get you to have a strong sense of purpose it will create remarkable mental, physical health and financial benefits. Physical benefits will include better sleep, protection against heart disease, and even a significantly reduced risk of dying of all causes.

Mental and emotional benefits include better relationships, higher quality of life and greater life satisfaction. Financial benefits allow you to provide and protect the quality of life for your family.

Very few people ever experience the power of life purpose that helps them to stay healthy, happy and living longer. You have to become emotional to motivate action that creates a strong sense of purpose and extraordinarily sustainable and powerful results.

When you connect your everyday actions with your deeply held values and beliefs – with your life purpose – even mundane actions take on a sense of importance and urgency.

That's right, mundane action that used to produce nothing is now moving in conjunction with your purpose. This is important for you to understand. Understanding your purpose/motivation gives you many valuable insights into the vision of wealth creation. It explains why you set goals, strive for achievement and power, why you have desires to be your greatest.

Learning about motivation is valuable because it helps you understand where motivation comes from, why it changes, what increases and decreases it, what aspects of it can and cannot be changed, and helps you answer the question of why some types of motivation are more beneficial than others.

Motivation reflects (reimagine) something unique about you and allows you to gain valued outcomes like improved performance, enhanced wellbeing, personal growth, or a sense of purpose. Motivation is a pathway to change your way of thinking, feeling, and behaving.

Finding ways to increase your motivation is crucial because it allows you to change behavior, develop competencies, be creative, set goals, grow interests, make plans, develop talents, and boost engagement.

Most people are working for the sole purpose of earning a living, or for achieving personal gain, and they often fail to provide fulfillment. That's where a sense of purpose comes in. The greater your purpose the more motivated you will feel to invest time and energy.

It is so important to know the difference between purpose and goals. A goal exists to serve your purpose, not act as your purpose. Purpose is the driving force behind your actions. It guides the goals that you set.

Your chosen purpose is often much greater than yourselves. It encompasses more than the sum of the goals you create as you work towards it.

Your chosen purpose reflects your values. Consciously living with purpose enables you to lead a values-based life. Our most effective actions are often anchored in your values. Embracing values-driven action is one way of knowing that you are on a path that is right for you.

Striving for a personally meaningful purpose provides you with direction. When you are clear of your purpose and the goals required to achieve that purpose, it makes you virtually unstoppable.

This level of clarity helps you connect with like-minded people who can amplify your potential. Clarity has a way of drawing the things you need into your life and cause harmful things to leave.

Purpose helps you stay focused on what truly matters. Being able to maintain mental clarity and avoid distractions, makes worries and challenges less daunting.

Knowing your purpose can lead you to your passion, and being passionate about your goals increases your drive to achieve them. As I said earlier, having meaning behind your actions can make even the most mundane aspects of your life feel brighter.

Knowing your purpose enables you to live and act with integrity. It becomes easier to behave in accordance with your core values because you know who you are, what you are and why you are performing the role you have chosen.

Your purpose is expressed in our thoughts, decisions, feelings and actions. A greater sense of purpose shapes you and your life, meaning you are better able to make an impact. This makes life highly gratifying.

Whatever your purpose may be, once you find it, own it and observe as your life takes shape around it. Finding your sense of purpose not only aids your journey, it determines the paths of those you lead, the destiny of your wealth creation and in some way, the future of the world.

When it comes to your self-motivation in behavioral change, your purposes also play a role in maintaining behavioral change over time. You can succeed in maintaining your long-term changes in behavior (e.g., investing, saving, wealth creation).

I need you to learn to see everything around you and your responses to it as a matter of your own choice, and having this perspective will be empowering and a great source of your ability to create wealth.

As you seek opportunities to invest, you will take initiative, set your own goals, and take an equal interest in helping others as well from your own inner experience. You are controlling and behaving with a strong sense of desire.

Now you understand that your focus determines your reality, and you have what it takes to shape your destiny beyond your dreams.

When you feel your behavior is something you initiate and regulate, you can make and sustain changes. This is in contrast to those, who at the other end of the spectrum, take on the victim of circumstances mentality

Things you may have heard before:

Everybody Knows:

You can't be all things to all people.

You can't do all things at once.

You can't do all things equally well.

You can't do all things better than everyone else.

Your humanity is showing just like everyone else's.

So:

You have to find out who you are, and be that.

You have to decide what comes first, and do that.

You have to discover your strengths, and use them.

You have to learn not to compete with others,

Because no one else is in the contest of *being you*.

Then:

You will have learned to accept your own uniqueness.

You will have learned to set priorities and make decisions.

You will have learned to live with your limitations.

You will have learned to give yourself the respect that is due.

And you'll be a most vital mortal.

Dare To Believe:

That you are a wonderful, unique person.

That you are a once-in-all-history event.

That it's more than a right, it's your duty, to be who you are.

That life is not a problem to solve, but a gift to cherish.

And you'll be able to stay one up on what used to get you down.

None of it sounds appealing to me. You have to be purposeful to think or talk things through carefully — it is also necessary that you weigh and measure.

Being deliberate is a skill. And mastering that skill will create the space for a higher level of performance when life presents its challenges.

What are the key attributes involved in being deliberate?

- You have a purpose you are passionate about.
- You have and will do your research.
- You believe it's worth pursuing.
- You are comfortable and it balances.
- You believe you have what it takes and the confidence to deliver it.
- You have sought the right input and support.
- You have thought it through with the right plans in place.

- You have made a commitment to yourself to hold you accountable.
- You are inspired and energized by the anticipation of the outcome.

This is going to happen for you no matter what obstacles you might encounter. You will just keep dancing until it rains.

Of course, when all this is said and done, you have to embrace the purpose and just do it. The mission of your focus will be the vision – you must know where you are going. People with vision can see their outcome before there is an outcome.

You have to begin to map at this level before there is anything tangible. If you cannot see an outcome here, it is not likely you can get what you want. Wealth creation is your vision.

Any wealth creation impacts your plan – This is the thought process, the ideas, the strategy, and tactics. It doesn't even have to be perfect. But it should be written down. Writing things down makes them real. It allows you to be held accountable either to yourself or to others (when or if we share our plans). And it has to be well enough designed

Finally, you must start. It doesn't have to be perfect action – it just has to be pointed generally in the right direction. People so often try and wait until the plan is perfect. In the meantime, the opportunity keeps moving – it doesn't stop and wait for you. So, if not now, when? Where is your vision?

Chapter Seven

Vision

What do you see? What do you think wealth creation is all about? We are now about to look at your focus in a different way. With the right focus, the right vision, all that you can imagine is possible.

The sole purpose of this book and this series is about making an impact, leaving a legacy, and having the resources to live the life you want. I want this new knowledge to work for you, building upon your dreams to create strategies for your long-term financial success.

As you learn and see that money is a predictable resource. More importantly, so can your time be. This book is designed for you to build and preserve wealth, giving you more time to get what you want out of life.

The task before you is easily related to mountain climbing. It's one thing to climb part of a mountain. It's another to reach the summit. Let's be clear there is nothing wrong with doing both.

Knowing that you are building personal or legacy wealth, your financial journey should be one that you can enjoy peace of mind, and the view from on top.

Done right, wealth creation comes with significant perks. But it also comes with complexity. A part of your wealth strategy optimizes your net worth by combining what your heart and mind want with sound financial vision.

Vision

Your most important asset is your ability to trust your vision. Understanding your viewpoint on complex financial decisions will require trust, experience, and perspective.

As you balance your needs today with your goals for the future you can begin to realize the big picture as you work to build, maintain, and transfer generational wealth.

Imagine having enough money to sustain your lifestyle for the rest of your life — and no longer needing to work to enjoy your passions and hobbies. Your focus helps get you there by setting incremental and adaptable goals.

When you get to a place of building meaningful wealth, you want to ensure it's sustained through any philanthropy or future generations. You have to make smart estate planning decisions so your wealth is preserved and passed on in ways you see fit.

It will be your vision that will see if your wealth is growing faster — or slower — than expected. Your goals and your priorities will ensure that your plans are flexible and adaptable to any unforeseen circumstances.

Have you ever been caught up than when you go right and everything else goes left, vision and focus becomes your built-in contingency plan to correct your course when needed.

I do not care how much you plan, life can change at the drop of a hat. And any change can quickly impact your two most valuable, predictable resources: money and time.

During these transitions, it's important to redefine your financial priorities and ensure your freedom to do the things you enjoy with the ones you care about.

You will need to build margins and add plenty of levers for adjustments as your situation changes.

Your purpose, your goals and your vision replaces financial guesswork with a clear, concise, and methodical plan. Your goal is to enable yourself to build, grow and preserve your finances to their full potential. The wisdom of this book is all about you having a steady focus to guide you through challenging circumstances.

"It's better to be an inch wide and a mile deep than a mile wide and an inch deep." —Anonymous

There is absolutely no strategy that can assure success or fully protect you from loss. Investing involves risk, and it is important to understand the risk and objectives of each strategy before investing. Past performance is no guarantee of future results.

However, with your new gain knowledge you now can make decisions on how to create wealth for your family and minimize the threat of loss.

It's extremely important having a vision, you see (pun intended) with the trials and tribulations that may come your way, when you have a clear vision of what you want to happen, you can make better decisions.

Please don't receive this negatively, most of our life is filled with uncertainty. This is especially true of the future. But if you can hold onto a vision of what's yet to come, you can boost your chances at achieving your dreams and being successful.

What is vision exactly?
How does it help, and what does it mean to have a vision?

Your vision is the act of your power of imagination. When you apply vision to the future, you can create a mental picture that can be used to direct your actions. Vision serves as a guide and can be used to provide a sense of purpose.

The fact is you will have to overcome roadblocks and hurdles on your journey to wealth creation. Challenges are inevitable. When you run into a wall or a hurdle, you need to know which way to go.

Vision provides you with something to look forward to and always work towards. It provides you with a reason to keep going, even when the times get tough.

The only way in my opinion to substantiate your goals is having a vision that places a purpose upon your goal-setting activities. Without an end goal or destination in mind, then you won't have a clear or defined path. You may never be focused at all.

I am writing about vision because it provides you the ability to achieve your goal, you can start by setting small, attainable goals as stepping stones. Each relatively little bit of success will help to continue propelling you forward on your bigger journey.

I talked about expectations earlier, I talked about setting goals and how it comes along with defining measurements of success. If you set a goal, how do you know when you've reached it if you don't have a way to define success? An overall life vision helps to set expectations accordingly.

The ability to focus – having a vision ensures that your life goals can remain in focus. When you are faced with a decision or distraction, you can ask yourself if it will help or hurt you in attaining your vision. This can offer you the means to move forward with intentional intention and alignment.

It's not always easy to deliver meaningful and purposeful goals in your life. You may even question yourself and your actions at times.

Your vision is a way to answer your own "why" of life. It gives you the reason for your actions, choices, hopes, and desires. It fills your daily activities with meaning and purpose.

You can strengthen your focus by creating a vision statement and vision board. I want to be careful how I communicate this because I do not want to sound like many of my colleagues who recommend a statement or board as if it is Sugar, Honey, Ice, Tea. It's not. Almost everybody has one…

Anyone can create their own vision statement, it is promoted everywhere. People can develop a personal vision statement just as most businesses do. Business entities have a common purpose for them to write and share a vision statement.

A vision statement for them is a written expression of the purpose and meaning behind their business model that's intended for stakeholders, including employees and even customers. It's their roadmap to success.

Wealth creation for you is going to require a strong vision statement that you are to write in the present tense, express an outcome that's achievable, and evokes emotion. Project into the future what you desire. It projects into the future by reimagining your destiny.

Yes I said to write it in present tense, it needs to also be forward-looking because that's what vision is. I previously gave you a vision of looking five or ten years into the future to understand what you hope to achieve by then. You can ask questions about what things will look like and/or the market you're operating in.

Many people attempt to move forward with an idea that has not been vetted. They will attempt to go all in without determining their current position. In order to know where you want to go, you should first assess where you are and the resources available.

There is something called an **OAS** statement. Objective, Advantage, and Scope.

Objective

Your objective of wealth creation is to make sure you have the money to achieve it all. Having a good financial plan means resources have been allocated towards achieving your goals in a systematic manner

Advantage

The benefits of wealth creation include an ability to effectively budget for costs, higher savings rates for retirement, and making prudent investment choices that will help you reach your financial goals

Scope

Wealth creation is the process of planning and managing personal financial activities such as income generation, spending, saving, investing, and protection. The process of managing one's wealth creation can be summarized in a budget or financial plan

As you clearly define what success looks like and how it will be measured for your family. It is your value standard, it's a good idea to look at models of things you would hope to emulate. It will provide inspiration or a better understanding of how you can get to where you want to be.

I know you have read this many times already to create measurable goals that are in line with your vision and communicate them to your circle of influence.

If the idea of vision statements and business goals excite you, then a career in business might be a part of your personal vision!

The bottom line: to accomplish your personal goals in life, having a vision is important. The approach and answer to the question of, "What is a vision?" could be different from one person to the next.

However, it will always entail a look into the future with a mental image of what's to come. Clearly defining your vision and referring back to it when you make your decisions with wealth creation will help you to achieve your goals.

Your vision can also consist of personal goals, physical health, career goals, educational goals, and any other aspects of life. No matter what aspect you choose to focus on, you can define and attain your vision with effort, determination, and focus!

The primary way of thinking about wealth is as individual possession, or a possession you earn and use to provide for your immediate care (i.e., your family).

In this view, wealth is the reward of effort and talent, and downstream of your supposed meritocracy. I say supposed because meritocracy is largely an illusion not vision.

You may at any given time be working towards achieving multiple wealth creation goals. Not all of these will be long-term goals like retirement.

You might need to reach some goals like saving for a new car or down payment for a new house much sooner. Depending on how near or far in the future a particular goal is, your risk-taking ability for different goals will vary.

As a result, you cannot rely on a single investment strategy to ensure that you stay on track to achieve all of these goals. So, you will need to implement different wealth creation strategies that are customized to each financial goal.

Even with the best vision you will have to put in time and effort to choose investments and determine the ideal asset allocation mix to reach your wealth creation goal.

You will manually select individual investments and figure out how to rebalance your investments periodically to generate optimal risk-adjusted returns.

Wealth creation is a continuous process. You need to make a plan and stick to it so that you can meet all your goals. Plus there is no one-size-fits-all wealth creation solution as each individual has unique goals, risk tolerance, etc.

So, choosing the right investment that can help you achieve your goals plays a key role in ensuring you succeed in creating wealth over time.

Please be aware that wealth creation will be greatly impacted by the lack of clarity. Your vision can experience blurriness and the reason will be lack of focus.

You may notice that on some days your vision is clearer and your decisions are on point and on other days it seems things are so blurry.

Do not commit yourself to a point of confusion, do not allow outside influences to sway or slow you down from your mission. Sometimes your vision is going to be as clear as can be and someone with a dark spirit shows up and you can hardly see anything.

Don't be surprised if you notice changes in the clarity of your vision during different times. Be careful, stress also can also cause vision concerns and, ironically, when experiencing problems it can create more stress.

The market is not doing well and you are experiencing great losses and you missed an opportunity to make other investments. This can be stressful, which can actually interfere with your vision.

As you continue to develop your financial vision it must be carefully crafted and articulated to provide a mutual guidance and appreciation for your wealth creation future.

Your vision will guide you in creating a direction for your wealth you will also create insight and clarity about who you are and what you care about.

Vision

Your financial vision provides both yourself and your household the ingredients for solid discernment and intuition in making the right financial decisions for your family and wealth creation for years to come.

Undoubtedly all of your lives will have changes, challenges and opportunities and a clarified, agreed upon and recorded vision serves to ensure you fully comprehend and understand the hopes and expectations for the future.

Chapter Eight

The Lens

Wealth creation is more than a concept. Wealth creation is sometimes nothing more than your mindset. All through this book and the series I have put before many things that show how you can change your financial course of life with "Real Steps". As I talk about focus and how important it is on your journey, it is time to consider the lens for which you view wealth creation.

Many people may find it difficult to accept some of the points I am going to state here, but the truth remains that people tend to see the world in a different light. There are really the ideas of Wealth vs. Poverty and the way the two classes see it. It is important to consider the mentality behind such thoughts, since becoming wealthy isn't such a bad idea.

What is the lens and mindset of your views of wealth and the world around you? Do you tend to see things from a wealthy or poverty view? The wealthy mindsets are positive about wealth creation and the world around them while poverty mindsets blame the world for their problems

The wealthy are used to taking charge of their financial lives. They know that there are a lot of financial hardships that already exist, but they don't dwell on it.

In fact they work hard to fix the aspects that they can fix and act responsibly for what happens to them. And for this reason many wealthy mindsets are philanthropists.

Poverty mindsets offer excuses and use the word “if” a lot. They tend to point fingers at this or that for the wrongs in their lives. They think that they have been wronged all along and try to play the victim every now and then. Poverty mindsets never take on the responsibility they can control their financial journey.

Here is something to chew on. Wealthy mindsets believe that poverty is the root of all evil while poverty mindsets believe money is the root of all evil. How you may see a thing impact your actions towards a thing.

Wealthy mindsets know that poverty can cause a man so much pain. They know that if poverty was eradicated or not in the picture, humanity would make more progress. Money is not evil to them. Rather, they see it as a means to an end in gaining all that they want in life. Money may not guarantee happiness, but it can make life easier and more comfortable to live in.

What I am really trying to get you to see is wealth creation and life when placed under a magnifying glass is greatly in large. Through the lens of your exposure, your experience, your desires and your focus you create your narrative.

Poverty mindsets think that money is the root of all evil and that rich people are dishonest and greedy. They do not see money for what it is — an avenue to attain more financial freedom. Rather they see it as a cause to the many headaches they are suffering. They will simply be okay with contentment and simplicity because they feel that wealth comes at such a high price.

Wealthy mindsets believe in taking action while poverty mindsets wait for everything to take place with the chance of them getting a portion. Wealthy mindsets believe you need to attract opportunities by working hard and taking action. They do not believe in gambling and chances of playing the lottery to become more prosperous.

They would rather go out there and solve problems or add value to the world around them. There is no point in waiting for God, government or certain institutions to offer them a lucky hand for them to become more prosperous.

Poverty mindsets believe in chance and luck or taking a gamble on almost everything that will come their way. They are would-be patrons of get-rich-quick schemes and the lottery. Rather than go out there to improve their chances, they will sit and wait for "almighty" factors to determine their fortunes.

Wealthy mindsets do not see formal education as a direct path to prosperity while poverty mindsets see a formal education as all you need to become wealthy

Wealthy mindsets know that you need more than a formal education to succeed in life. Actually, many top performers and wealthy people had to work hard, persevere and acquire specific knowledge along the way to become who they are.

Wealthy mindsets do not see the world from a linear angle, but rather from a diversified angle of making prosperity from diverse means. It really is not about the means, after all, but the end.

Poverty mindsets are stuck with the thought that you can only become somebody and rich after you have attained a degree or gone through a prestigious institution of knowledge. However, this thought only keeps them prisoners of mediocrity and staying on the average line. This is the lens that has held back generations of people who have had wealth at their fingertips.

Point Made Right!

Man I hope that I open the financial lens of your mind to bring another repeated process to the forefront. Through your lens you must know that managing your wealth goes well beyond just crunching numbers.

Yea, there are plenty of numbers when it comes to wealth creation, but there is also an element of art that goes into making sure your wealth works for your specific and often-changing needs, goals, and overall lifestyle.

That's why I am trying to get you to look through the lens of your life as I cover both the math and the art of wealth creation with best practices and realistic tactics you can use to create and manage your wealth in a way that works for your life — no matter where it may take you.

You have to see the process of managing your wealth and it's multifaceted and consists of practice like budgeting, saving, investing, and even (wisely) spending your capital.

Okay, I am throwing capital in the conversation, capital is mostly interchangeable with money, and most of you will generate it via a salary, business profits, investments, and other common financial sources.

This is so important, your dreams of legacy, your goal and how you manage your wealth and maximizing the value of your capital so you can apply it to your goals. Because, as you know, goals — whether you're thinking about next year's vacation or how you can retire earlier to spend more time with your family — require funds. The lens!

And these goals are just one of the things you must know before getting into the nitty-gritty of creating your wealth. First and foremost, to manage and create your wealth effectively you must know why you're managing it.

What do you want your money to do? Prioritize a list of short- and long-term goals. This list is something you'll probably want to manage activity, just like you will your wealth — more on that later. The lens!

In order to effectively manage your wealth, you also need a clear understanding of all the assets that make up your wealth. Especially important elements of the wealth equation that you'll want to get cozy with are your income (money in), your expenditures (money out), any investments that you've made (in the stock market or elsewhere), and any debts you might hold (from credit cards, student loans, mortgages, and more).

Do you ever consider getting intimately familiar with how these all play together in your financial life? By doing so, you will discover that it will help you have a better understanding of where you are and inform you of what is the best process for you to create and manage your wealth to meet your goals.

How do you see your personal net worth? Have you taken a look at all of your assets? Have you simplified who assets? What is in your portfolio? Did you know that your net worth should change weekly? The lens!

Know that your net worth is only a calculation of the value of everything you own — minus what you owe (debt). Tracking net worth is important because it's a widely-recognized number that can be compared against benchmarks to see where you stand. It can always change.

Once you know your net worth, you can watch it over time to get an idea of how healthy your wealth creation is and whether it's growing (usually good) or shrinking (usually not good). It's also smart to keep an eye on your net worth after big life or financial changes to make sure your goals are still what you want them to be, that they're still achievable, and that you're still on target to hit them. The lens!

Listen, your net worth may be a big deal, but it doesn't have to be a big deal to understand and monitor your net worth. After all poverty mindsets rather check and monitor their credit score over their net worth. Go figure! The lens!

In the last chapter "Vision" I asked you what do you see? The lens for which you are making your decision about your wealth creation serves as a guide as you zoom in on your focus. This next piece will again assist you in reimagining your wealth creation.

I often talk about the basic accounts needed to get you on the right path; checking, saving, and investment accounts. A part of your wealth creation foundation is having a retirement account. By you reading this and you haven't yet, one of the best ways to create and manage your wealth so it works for you is starting a retirement account.

These are some of the very basic things I want you to put in your life. One of the easy ways to invest in your future is to participate in your employer's 401(k) plan. When doing so, be sure to invest up to the company's match. Let me explain, your company will match you dollar for dollar up to on average of 6%, this is free money, so you be sure to invest 6%, no more than that,

If that's not an option, then you must set up an Individual Retirement Account (IRA). For either, you should be able to set up an automatic monthly contribution. It's important that you actively revisit this contribution regularly — at the least, when you change jobs — to make sure you're putting in as much as you're comfortable with as regularly as you can. Are you seeing this? By what lens?

Your goodness, I know you are tired of hearing about this one. Establishing a realistic budget is still my go too. Yes, at its core, a budget is a way your money is tracked in versus money out; when it comes to creating and managing your wealth, it can be much, much more than that.

Through your lens you can see that you have a thorough (and realistic!) budget and it is really a starting point for reaching all of those goals that require money to achieve. A budget gives you the information you need to know to reach your goals when you want to reach them.

A budget forces you to think intentionally, focus intentionally about your financial habits, and once you have one set up it empowers you to stress less about expenses and feel confident in your future plans.

Once you're on your way to a functioning budget that helps you see how your money works and put plans in place for its future allocation, you must have some important rules of thumb to remember about those expenses that we all have to think about.

I know that everyone's priorities will be different, but typically they'll include saving toward emergency savings accounts, paying down debts, putting money in retirement accounts, etc.

You should notice that my advice is going to be put in several different ways throughout this book: Review your budget regularly and revise as needed! Your income as well as your goals will change with time, and so should your budget to stay true to life. Remember, your income is not your wealth.

When it comes to creating and managing your wealth, time is one of your best friends so invest early and often. The more time your wealth has to accumulate in investments — or high-yield savings accounts — the longer returns and compounding interest have to add up. The lens!

In fact, with enough time, the interest and dividends earned on what you put away can even exceed the amount you put in. It's this fact that makes starting early so important when it comes to your retirement account. The Lens!

In our opinion, everyone should try investing in the stock market as a means of wealth management and growth. It's important to remember that time is the name of the game, so you should be willing to leave whatever you invest in the market for at least five to ten years.

The best place to get started in the stock market is with affordable index funds and exchange-traded funds (ETFs). These types of stocks enable you to purchase a variety of stocks in a single transaction, which may mitigate your returns but can also mitigate the risks and management tasks that come with individual stocks.

Rebalance your portfolio as needed, what I am saying here is for you to review your portfolio's allocations and adjust them (by buying or selling certain assets) to line up with your current goals and risk tolerance. Once you have a clear overview of portfolio performance, you can actually do this quite effectively.

I do recommend that you are rebalancing on a regular basis — at least twice a year is recommended — keeps your portfolio diverse, gives you a chance to make sure you're still happy with your goals, and provides insight into whether anything needs to be tweaked to meet those goals. This is focusing through your lens for what you desire.

Your rebalancing should lead to diversifying your investments. Your portfolio diversification simply means investing in various kinds of assets, but you know this already.

Howevcr, the reason diversification is always recommended to wealth creators is that it protects your portfolio from sudden losses that can impact a single market at any given time.

A well-balanced portfolio contains a blend of assets that align with your risk tolerance while still generating returns that attribute to your goals.

Diversity can apply to what kinds of companies and industries you're invested in, what areas of the world you're invested in, and what kinds of assets you're invested in. And, it's an exciting time to be a wealth creator because of a new asset class on the market: Digital assets.

In most cases, digital asset investments are those that exist in and are derived from the digital world. Right now, the most well-known digital asset is cryptocurrency.

Now is the perfect time to add in digital investments while you're managing your wealth and thoughtfully diversifying your portfolio.

You must learn how to focus on the elements of your wealth that you can actively create and manage and not stress out too much over the rest.

You should prioritize these elements over which you have the most control: How much you save, how much you spend, how you choose to allocate your assets, and how you behave with your investments.

Once you're comfortable with your system for managing the above, you might want to consider the things that impact your finances over which you have some control: Your income, your source(s) of income, and how long you'll be generating that income. The lens!

Finally, there are elements that impact your wealth that you can of course keep an eye on, but over which you have no control: Taxes, market performance, and governmental rulings that affect your returns.

The best overall thing you can do to create and manage your wealth effectively is to focus on what you can manage and forget what you can't.

What's better than being able to manage your wealth to achieve your goals in this lifetime? Managing your wealth so that it helps your heirs achieve their goals even after your lifetime.

Often, the important documents upon which your wealth is built — deeds, contracts, and more — are left out of the wealth management conversation.

However, it's important that those documents are kept safe and end up in the right hands after your death if you want to ensure that your wealth keeps working for your future generations.

Creating and managing your wealth for your own goals as well as for future generations doesn't have to be a heavy burden.

The lens for which you can see. Get focus…

Chapter Nine

Now Focus

You are becoming a wealth creator, directing your focus toward where it needs to go is a critical task of wealth creation. The talent here lies in your ability to shift attention to the right place at the right time, identifying trends, emerging realities, and opportunities.

There will be issues as you pursue your goals. You will make your choices about where to focus based on your perception of what matters to your wealth creation goals.

You will have an extra load of responsibility. You will be guiding not just your own focus but, to a large extent, everyone else's in your household. As you "focus" be careful about showing a one-pointedness on your overall results, or on a particular strategy, a single-pointedness may not be enough.

Being this wealth creator you are going to need strengths in three areas of focus: self (inner), people (other), and system (outer) awareness. Inner (self) focus attunes you to your emotions and intuitions, guiding values and better decisions. We talked about your values and your purpose earlier.

Other (people) focus smooths your connections to the people in your lives. This can be your greatest challenge or your greatest asset. And the outer (system) focus lets you navigate the larger world. Wealth creation involves the whole world of finance and how you focus is important.

But the challenge goes beyond that. The key is finding balance, and knowing when to use the right kind of focus at the right time. When you take your experience in focusing along with that on emotional intelligence and performance, this triple focus emerges as your hidden driver of excellence.

You have it inside of you by now. If not, read the book again. In fact, read all of them again. Now if you are not careful with the balance you can/will be blinded by the prize. You can see where single-point focus can go wrong,

It's almost as if you are micromanaging yourself, constantly second-guessing everything, changing processes that didn't meet your standards even though they were perfectly fine. You could always find something to criticize but nothing to praise. Your steadfast focus on the negative demoralized your household—now they seek to quit.

The failure here is not in reaching the goal, but in connecting with people inside your household. The just-get-it-done mode runs over family concerns and is a bad focus.

You need your family at some point to have a keen focus on goals that matter, the talent to continually learn how to do even better, and the ability to look away from distractions. Innovation, productivity, and growth depend on such high-performers.

When you are fixated on a goal, whatever is relevant to that point of focus gets priority. Focus is not just selecting the right thing but also saying no to the wrong ones; focus goes too far when it says no to the right things, too.

If you don't have self-awareness when you get hooked by the drive to achieve a goal, that's when you lose empathy and return to autopilot. How you used to do things in the past that did not work.

As a wealth creator you need self-awareness to assess your own strengths and weaknesses, and so surround yourself with a team of people whose strengths in those core abilities complement your own. This means inner focus.

Of course that doesn't mean you can ignore other concerns, like market trends or innovation, to meet changing demands. But realize the same attention skills that can help manage one's own emotions and relationships can help you stay more flexible and allow for better outer focus.

Wealth creation mindfulness is you constantly questioning and listening; inquiry, probing, and reflecting—gathering insights and perspectives from other (wealthy) people. This is expanding your circle of connection beyond your comfort zone.

Your focus builds on the basic mechanics of your mental life. Self-awareness, which fosters self-management, and empathy, the basis for skill in relationships, are fundamentals of emotional intelligence.

I am talking about broader bands of focus as you regard the financial world around you. All of this can be boiled down to inner, other, and outer focus. If you are going to get results you need all three kinds of focus.

However, let's not forget what I talked about earlier in this book all of the various areas that have an impact on your ability to focus.

Procrastination

I first wanted to show elements that have a negative impact on you. Fear is one factor that contributes to procrastination. This can involve a fear of failure, a fear of making mistakes, or even a fear of success.

If you are afraid of success because you secretly believe that you don't deserve it, it is important to realize that your self-handicapping might be keeping you from achieving your goals. By addressing the fear that is keeping you from getting started head on, you can begin to overcome your procrastination habit.

You have to start by creating a to-do list with things that you would like to accomplish. If necessary, put a date next to each item if there is a deadline that you need to meet.

I know this sounds like the same old things to do, but remember there are two purposes here. Wealth Creation for generation and the focus necessary to meet that goal are your purposes.

When you are saving and investing it is not difficult to determine the amount that you will use weekly or monthly, it's the return that you will receive.

So when you are trying to set estimates on how long each goal will take to complete, be realistic, and then double that number so that you don't fall into the cognitive trap of underestimating how long each goal will take.

When you are faced with hard times, you might feel daunted, intimidated, or even hopeless when you look at the sheer amount of effort required. At this point, take individual items on your list and break them down into a series of steps. Much like I am doing with this series.

If you need to create a budget first, what steps do you need to follow? If you are planning a big family event, what are the things you need to do and what supplies do you need to obtain?

Once you have created a list detailing the process you need to go through in order to accomplish your goals, you can start working on individual "intentional steps."

As you start to tackle items on your list, pay attention to when thoughts of procrastination start to creep into your mind. If you find yourself thinking "I don't feel like doing this now" or "I'll have time to work on this later," then you need to recognize that you are about to procrastinate.

When you feel tempted to procrastinate, don't give in to the urge. Instead, force yourself to spend at least a few minutes working on your vision. You might discover that it is easier to complete once you get started.

Now Focus!

It's hard to get any real results when you keep turning your attention to what's on television or you keep checking your friends' Facebook status updates. Assign yourself a period of time during which you turn off all distractions—such as music, television, and social networking sites—and use that time to focus all of your attention on wealth creation.

Once you have completed a goal (or even a small portion of a larger goal), it is important to reward yourself for your efforts. Reward does not mean to sabotage your efforts or purposes with the mentality of I deserve this.

It’s okay to give yourself the opportunity to indulge in something that you find fun and enjoyable, whether it's attending a sporting event, playing a video game, watching your favorite TV show, or looking at pictures on a social sharing site.

Breaking the procrastination habit isn't easy. The urge to put things off can be strong, especially when there are so many things around you to provide fun and entertaining distractions.

While procrastination might not be something you can avoid entirely, becoming cognizant of the reasons why you procrastinate and how to overcome those tendencies can help.

By implementing these strategies, you might find that it is easier to put your nose to the grindstone and get started on those wealth creation goals.

Contentment

Remember, I believe that contentment is an enemy of your focus. I want you to be able to see why you cannot be content; why you can only surge ahead or collapse. Yet, most people do not see how this same principle works. In fact, we are taught that contentment is a big virtue, that it is a state of satisfaction attained with some success.

After all our reasonable material needs are fulfilled, we are told, we must not yearn for more and more. Contentment is stillness, it is peace, and it is stability. It is a nicer word for falling behind. If ambition is a capacity for unhappiness, contentment is the talent for happiness.

Maybe because I grew up poor, I have known many content types. I myself was one once, but then the zombies came for me. I refused to be dead.

I have known people who have escaped their circumstances through hard work and then grown content. People who have gotten a great break in their lives and embraced a peaceful life of not wanting more than a comfortable life.

Most of them are bitter today. Contentment, it turns out, does not lead to happiness.

When it comes down to wealth creation you must have a focus to accumulate wealth. If you are not moving forward towards it, you are slipping backwards.

Contentment may have a middle ground. The very poor cannot possess it. It emerges from a material state that is not very low. As the content stays still, others around them prosper. There are lessons to be learned. Prosperity is inflationary to wealth creation.

Some could say defining the quality of the content types is bitterness. You could be both content and successful at the same time. So you think your happiness may emerge from your contentment. In reality, it emerged from superficial success.

Listen, if you remain still, you rot. If you do not have ambitions, you can be destroyed by a sudden phenomenon, like a pandemic. But then should the fear of destruction change your character?

The problem is not in the scale of success or even the devaluation of the middle ground. Contentment is bliss, so long as the people who have it also have the humor to tolerate being overtaken by the restless. Those who refuse to remain still.

Remember here I am talking about how contentment is an enemy to your ability to focus to create wealth. Focus has a few sources of enemies that we often become complacent with in our day to day lives that we are unable to recognize the damage it causes.

I must go here because many of my readers will be questioning why I did not incorporate the spiritual aspect of this thing called contentment. This is the lesson, regardless of your faith or lack thereof, this is my strongest argument that contentment is a problem towards wealth creation.

Why is contentment a problem?

Biblically, when you consider the principles of the bible it is speaking in terms of godly character. As with most aspects of godly character, contentment is a middle path between two unacceptable extremes, complacency and covetousness.

In this world contentment is rare–more and more people are rarely satisfied with their relationships, with their possessions, with their place in life.

We are complacent when it comes to our morals–not often diligent in fulfilling our duties, or we are greedy when it comes to desiring more power and money and higher positions for ourselves. Even this greediness has absolutely nothing to do with our desire for wealth creation. But though we often waver between complacency and covetousness, we seldom find contentment much less remain there for any length of time.

Expectations

Yes, expectations have let many, if not most people down. But you need to consider what expectations are. It is a want, a desire, a belief, or emotional anticipation you have about a future vision of yourself, an event, or action.

The future belief can be short term (5 minutes or a day from now), medium term (a week or a month from now), or long term (years from now).

I tell my clients often that you do have to be careful because expectations can also be realistic or unrealistic, and it's usually the "pie in the sky," "airy-fairy" expectations that cause us hurt, suffering, and frustration. It is the unrealistic side of your expectations that brings pain.

When you have expectations about anything – yourself, your friends and family, wealth creation, or life in general. Having an expectation is like having a wannabe reality you look forward to manifesting and actualizing.

An example of a realistic expectation would be that you expect to start a new job on November 3rd because that's what the date on your contract with your new employer states. This expectation is like an agreement between you and your boss – you both agreed on your starting date.

Another example is you agreeing to owning shares of a particular stock every single month. With this investment you agree to never withdraw or sell any share. Your expectation is the wealth you created allows this to fall into place with the commitment of $100 a month.

On the other hand, before I give you an example of an unrealistic expectation, let's look at this way for clarity. They are rigid. They don't leave room for changing circumstances or allow you or others to be flexible.

Sometimes the expectations might seem reasonable, fair, and realistic, but your experience reveals they can't be met. Your expectations can also create more problems than they solve.

There's only one person in this world you can truly change—yourself—and even that takes a tremendous amount of effort. The only way that people change is through the desire and wherewithal to change themselves.

Still, it's tempting to try to change someone who doesn't want to change, as if your sheer will and desire for them to improve will change them (as it has you). You might even actively choose people with problems, thinking that you can "fix" them. Let go of this faulty expectation. Build your life around genuine, positive people, and avoid problematic people that bring you down.

When you expect things, you believe that something will happen in one way, but things don't always go according to our plans, or you expected more than what was realistically possible. When the expectation doesn't become reality, you feel disappointment and eventually even resentment.

This should not be hard to believe that most people do not expect to ever experience financial freedom or wealth creation. Their financial lives are caught with earning six figures and living their best life. Whatever that is for them, this should not be you after these Wealth Creation books.

One of my mentors once explained to me the power of unmet expectations is so significant – it negatively impacts how we see ourselves, the people around us, and the world.

Having expectations (aka premeditated resentments) leads you down the road of disappointments. But why do we have expectations in the first place? Are they something we learn? Are they something we intrinsically have?

Expectations are rooted in experiences you have with:

Yourself
Your folks
Your family
Your friends
Your peers and colleagues
Your mentors
Media and society

Reflection

As in the previous chapters, I want to elaborate on how beneficial your strategy to focus on wealth creation is to you. Nothing else, this is about you reimagining yourself from your past experiences by considering how you were affected by or have seen wealth around as you reflect back.

Why is reflection important for your wealth creation?

Reflection — is a process where you learn to review or even describe how your financial life has been in the past and how it changed, and how it very well may relate to your future learning experiences with money.

Please understand that it is a skill that often goes undervalued in our life experiences and is packed with content for learning. I reflect back to a time in my life that I was introduced to "Soft Butter", it made an impression on my life.

As a kid I was always in trouble, growing up poor I was limited in my experience and knowledge regarding basic foods.

We received welfare food in the seventies, powdered eggs, powdered milk, cheese (pound for pound the best cheese ever) and butter. Oh, I cannot leave out the yellow grain grits, not buttered or cheese grits – YELLOW.

So this doctor decided to pour into me by allowing me to work with him on Saturdays at his home. Every Saturday morning I would outside work in his yard, I would occasionally peep in the house and watch them eat breakfast.

He had two daughters and they would always catch me peeping in the window as they ate. On one of those mornings he came out and invited me in for breakfast. What a life experience it was for me. They had fresh sliced baked bread and took a knife and spread something over it, I first thought it was some kind of jelly, but it wasn't, it was soft butter.

Oh my goodness, I can recall the sweetness of the favor at this moment, the impact was there at the time but not truly realized until I reflected back to that moment. I do recall going back home and sharing that experience with my family only to be laughed at.

Then I begin to recognize the frequency of this commercial that played and again listen to my family laugh at me. That commercial was "Parkay – Butter – Parkaaay" I believe Deacon Jones was in one of them, it was clearly a reflection that gave me a vision outside of poverty.

However, reflection is important, it helps to make sense of and grow from a learning experience, and it should be a practice that if you are focusing on wealth creation that you develop. Let me be clear, reflecting is an important practice across many various disciplines including job performance, nursing, business, the sciences and more.

Therefore you should be exposing yourself to continuous reflective thinking practices so that you can become "creator" and not "consumers" of wealth.

Listen, I believe there will be a phenomenon in which new and unfamiliar thinking approaches through the application, remixing or integration of previous knowledge, skills, strategies, and dispositions that will create habits of the mind that leads to the success of wealth creation..

Your goal with reflection is putting many perspectives into play with each other in order to produce your insight. Simply looking forward to goals you might attain, as well as a casting backward to see where you have been.

When you reflect/reimagine, you thus project and review, often putting the projections and the reviews in sync with each other, and working to discover what you know, what you have learned, and what you might understand.

I know that just talking about reflection can be a set-up to failure, another sound good feel good moment that leads to only a 72 hour knowledge high.

After all your reflection is what you see in the mirror. But there are other things that bounce back at you are also reflections — light waves, sound waves, even your thoughts.

Intentionally Intentional

I believe that what people actually and precisely mean to "acting with intention" or being "intentional" is that they are proclaiming to be intentionally intentional. Intentional living is something that has caught on in the past few years.

People want to do work that has meaning and live out a purpose. Being a better money manager and wealth creator can be looked at the same way.

Wealth is not something that you just hope into, it is more about how you handle money. I must admit that some days are just on the impulse of people. There is no rhythm or rhyme to the course of the day as they move through it.

Being intentional with your money not only helps prevent lifestyle inflation, but it is also a key component of creating wealth within a budget that works for you. Let me define intentional as simply being "done on purpose." In other words, when you do something intentionally you mean to do it.

Likewise intentional spending, saving and investing is when you spend, save and invest money with purpose. It's when you're deliberate and mindful in your decisions. Intentional spending, saving and investing, is the opposite of impulse spending, saving and investing.

I could only hope that by now, you've probably begun to understand the benefits of being intentional with your money.

But what does intentional spending, saving and investing really mean? If you're like most people, you tend to put off thinking about financial matters until an emergency pops up or something needs to be purchased.

With inflation rates currently skyrocketing through the roof all over the world, now's a good time to stop waiting for an emergency and start being more intentionally intentional about where your money is going.

So many people believe that it's always more, more money and their most important job is to figure out how to get paid more. I completely disagree with that idea.

Let's look beyond the obviousness of income to say your most important job is to figure out how to live on less than what you earn. It sounds so intimidating, but it's feasible if you look at things holistically and start with purpose.

A few questions here:

- How often do you buy things on impulse or when you didn't mean to?
- How often are you tempted and overcome by the amount of deliciousness at the checkout in the grocery store?
- How many times have you grabbed that candy bar, even though you don't mean to?
- Did you know that the same impulse buying scenario can be intentional as well though?

Some of you will make a conscious choice to set aside a certain amount each month specifically for impulse buys and you don't go over that amount, then you are managing your money intentionally. But this money is not for wealth creation.

However, being intentional is all about making the decisions and sticking to them. You made a choice to set aside money that you can spend impulsively. You made the choice. Make the choice of saving and investing. Your intentional spending, saving and investing means you are being aware of where your money is going, and putting it towards things of real value.

Do some soul searching to find out exactly what you value.

For example, I value giving and generosity as well as families. I intentionally put my money toward a ministry that specializes in ministering to families. I have no issue giving to this ministry because it aligns with my values.

Some of you may value eating clean or sustainably. This usually costs more money than the cheap grocery store items that are filled with chemicals so it's important to make a conscious decision to put your money toward it. Right? The same is true to wealth creation.

You may have a passion for caring for the environment and not being overly wasteful. This may prevent you from drinking single-serve pod coffee and instead opt for more expensive fair trade coffee.

No matter what your values are, be confident in them. They are a part of who you are and should be reflected in what you do with your money.

It can be hard to figure out your values, I value being able to teach people how to manage their money and create wealth, but I didn't develop that passion by being passive about it. It took some work determining what I value.

No one can or should decide what you value for you. However, I hope that I can help you get there. Now go to one of your favorite places, a place where you can relax and clear your mind without being interrupted. Are you there yet? If not, stop reading until you actually do this.

Now, try and clear your mind of everything else that is going on around you. Lastly, relax. There will be no right or wrong answers when it comes to your values. Just own them.

Think back on your life, identify the following five things:

When were you most satisfied?
When were you the happiest?
What activities make you the proudest?
What do you really desire for you?
What commitments have you made that you value?

Purpose

Your financial goals are a target to aim for when managing your money. It does involve saving, spending, earning, or even investing. Wealth creation requires that you have a clear picture of what you're aiming for, working towards your target may not be easy. I just talked about how your goals should be measurable, specific, and time-oriented.

Let me get this out of the way. Having an emergency fund or saving for emergencies is one of the only goals that is a necessity. It should be the first one you should set, regardless of your situation. Life is unpredictable, and it's important to be prepared.

But please realize this is not wealth creation, it's a part of the foundation. When something unexpected and expensive occurs, emergency funds are there to keep you from suffering the financial blow.

Paying off debts is not a financial goal. It is your obligation and no one feels comfortable knowing that they owe large sums of money. And because the amount you owe is already a specific number, paying off debt can easily be eliminated.

Making every monthly payment on time is not enough, your best way to make real progress is to stop borrowing. Adding to your debt will only push you away from your ability to create wealth, so it's important to stay strong and diligent.

Buying a home is a financial goal right now. Whether you're saving for a down payment or working to pay off a mortgage, homeownership is one of the largest financial targets to aim for. Your life purpose consists of the central motivating aims of your life—the reasons you get up in the morning.

Purpose can guide life decisions, influence behavior, shape goals, offer a sense of direction, and create meaning. For some people, purpose is connected to vocation—meaningful, satisfying work.

For others, their purpose lies in their responsibilities to their family or friends. Others seek meaning through spirituality or religious beliefs. Some people may find their purpose clearly expressed in all these aspects of life.

Purpose will be unique for everyone; what you identify as your path may be different from others. What's more, your purpose can actually shift and change throughout life in response to the evolving priorities and fluctuations of your own experiences.

Some people feel hesitant about pursuing their life purpose because they worry that it sounds like a self-serving or selfish quest. However, true purpose is about recognizing your own gifts and using them to contribute to the world—whether those gifts are playing beautiful music for others to enjoy, helping friends solve problems, or simply bringing more joy into the lives of those around you.

Now, I will start out by asking you a few questions. Who are you? Seriously, who are you? Who are you as the provider? Who are you as a visionary? We are still in the rhythm of Wealth Creation The Focus, we must talk about purpose and purpose in a different way.

For most people it is in our nature to strive, to want, and move in a direction of something we desire and deem valuable. I honestly believe that your nature is to become a link or the first link to generational wealth and legacy transfer. This is your reason for purpose, to focus on something bigger than yourself.

Purpose is connection to a goal bigger than yourself; self-organizing aims that guides you and imbues even the simplest actions with relevance and meaning. It goes beyond a simple goal or objective because it's focused on the long-term and on a deeper meaning. It is all about finding and engaging your life purpose.

If I can get you to have a strong sense of purpose it will create remarkable mental, physical health and financial benefits. Physical benefits will include better sleep, protection against heart disease, and even a significantly reduced risk of dying of all causes.

Mental and emotional benefits include better relationships, higher quality of life and greater life satisfaction. Financial benefits allow you to provide and protect the quality of life for your family.

Vision

Done right wealth creation comes with significant perks. But it also comes with complexity. A part of your wealth strategy optimizes your net worth by combining what your heart and mind want with sound financial vision.

Your most important asset is your ability to trust your vision. Understanding your viewpoint on complex financial decisions will require trust, experience, and perspective.

As you balance your needs today with your goals for the future you can begin to realize the big picture as you work to build, maintain, and transfer generational wealth.

Imagine having enough money to sustain your lifestyle for the rest of your life — and no longer needing to work to enjoy your passions and hobbies. Your focus helps get you there by setting incremental and adaptable goals.

When you get to a place of building meaningful wealth, you want to ensure it's sustained through any philanthropy or future generations. You have to make smart estate planning decisions so your wealth is preserved and passed on in ways you see fit.

It will be your vision that will see if your wealth is growing faster — or slower — than expected. Your goals and your priorities will ensure that your plans are flexible and adaptable to any unforeseen circumstances.

Have you ever been caught up than when you go right and everything else goes left, vision and focus becomes your built-in contingency plan to correct your course when needed. I do not care how much you plan, life can change at the drop of a hat. And any change can quickly impact your two most valuable, predictable resources: money and time.

During these transitions, it's important to redefine your financial priorities and ensure your freedom to do the things you enjoy with the ones you care about. You will need to build margins and add plenty of levers for adjustments as your situation changes.

Your purpose, your goals and your vision replaces financial guesswork with a clear, concise, and methodical plan. Your goal is to enable yourself to build, grow and preserve your finances to their full potential. The wisdom of this book is all about you having a steady focus to guide you through challenging circumstances.

"It's better to be an inch wide and a mile deep than a mile wide and an inch deep." —Anonymous

There is absolutely no strategy that can assure success or fully protect you from loss. Investing involves risk, and it is important to understand the risk and objectives of each strategy before investing. Past performance is no guarantee of future results.

However, with your new gain knowledge you now can make decisions on how to create wealth for your family and minimize the threat of loss. It's extremely important having a vision, you see (pun intended) with the trials and tribulations that may come your way, when you have a clear vision of what you want to happen, you can make better decisions.

Please don't receive this negatively, most of our life is filled with uncertainty. This is especially true of the future. But if you can hold onto a vision of what's yet to come, you can boost your chances at achieving your dreams and being successful. What is vision exactly? How does it help, and what does it mean to have a vision?

Your vision is the act of your power of imagination. When you apply vision to the future, you can create a mental picture that can be used to direct your actions. Vision serves as a guide and can be used to provide a sense of purpose.

The fact is you will have to overcome roadblocks and hurdles on your journey to wealth creation. Challenges are inevitable. When you run into a wall or a hurdle, you need to know which way to go.

Vision provides you with something to look forward to and always work towards. It provides you with a reason to keep going, even when the times get tough.

The only way in my opinion to substantiate your goals is having a vision that places a purpose upon your goal-setting activities. Without an end goal or destination in mind, then you won't have a clear or defined path. You may never be focused at all.

Lens

Here is something to chew on. Wealthy mindsets believe that poverty is the root of all evil while poverty mindsets believe money is the root of all evil. How you may see a thing impacts your actions towards a thing.

Wealthy mindsets know that poverty can cause a man so much pain. They know that if poverty was eradicated or not in the picture, humanity would make more progress. Money is not evil to them. Rather, they see it as a means to an end in gaining all that they want in life. Money may not guarantee happiness, but it can make life easier and more comfortable to live in.

What I am really trying to get you to see is wealth creation and life when placed under a magnifying glass is greatly in large.

Through the lens of your exposure, your experience, your desires and your focus you create your narrative.

Poverty mindsets think that money is the root of all evil and that rich people are dishonest and greedy. They do not see money for what it is — an avenue to attain more financial freedom. Rather they see it as a cause of the many headaches they are suffering. They will simply be okay with contentment and simplicity because they feel that wealth comes at such a high price.

Wealthy mindsets believe in taking action while poverty mindsets wait for everything to take place with the chance of them getting a portion. Wealthy mindsets believe you need to attract opportunities by working hard and taking action. They do not believe in gambling and chances of playing the lottery to become more prosperous.

They would rather go out there and solve problems or add value to the world around them. There is no point in waiting for God, government or certain institutions to offer them a lucky hand for them to become more prosperous.

Poverty mindsets believe in chance and luck or taking a gamble on almost everything that will come their way. They are would-be patrons of get-rich-quick schemes and the lottery. Rather than go out there to improve their chances, they will sit and wait for "almighty" factors to determine their fortunes.

Wealthy mindsets do not see formal education as a direct path to prosperity while poverty mindsets see a formal education as all you need to become wealthy

Wealthy mindsets know that you need more than a formal education to succeed in life. Actually, many top performers and wealthy people had to work hard, persevere and acquire specific knowledge along the way to become who they are.

Wealthy mindsets do not see the world from a linear angle, but rather from a diversified angle of making prosperity from diverse means. It really is not about the means, after all, but the end.

Poverty mindsets are stuck with the thought that you can only become somebody and rich after you have attained a degree or gone through a prestigious institution of knowledge. However, this thought only keeps them prisoners of mediocrity and staying on the average line. This is the lens that has held back generations of people who has had wealth at their fingertips.

Now Get Out of Your Own Way

I know you know many people who will stand in your way if you let them. Sometimes, you're even the person in the way. You don't have to block yourself, though. You can be the reason all of your dreams come true when you are focused. Get out of your own way, so you aren't self-sabotaging yourself.

You can't complain that you didn't get what you wanted when you were not willing to put forth the effort. Taking a risk may be necessary to get results. It's time to break the cycle of holding yourself back and, instead, be accountable.

Part of how to get out of your own way is to start with a clean and clear mindset. Stop beating yourself up for your previous mistakes. Forget the times you set a goal but failed to achieve it. This time, focus on what you can do differently to change the outcome.

We have already talked about creating SMART goals: a goal that is specific, measurable, achievable, realistic, and timely. By doing this, you'll set yourself up for future success. And from this clean and clear mindset, you will be able to reposition yourself for that next level.

With a little bit, not a lot of focus, you will know how to get out of your own way because you will be too busy taking action that will lead you to greater heights.

Keep your eye on the prize to keep you motivated, to keep you accountable.

Ask yourself why you choose a particular goal.

What is the result you want?

Are your intentions pure, or is there ego involved?

How will your life change and improve once you reach that goal?

Focus on the why. This will prevent you from simply giving up on wealth creation. Having the right plan in place is one way to help you get out of your own way.

You are worth so much more than you realize. By knowing what you excel at, you can optimize yourself to master those great traits. It's about bringing out the best in you. If you bring the best version of yourself to the world each day, you'll have a significant impact on your life. You will feel a sense of fulfillment and accomplishment that enriches you.

We all have weak areas, don't let them hold you back. Identify them and decide how to get out of your own way despite their existence. If your weaknesses are more of a character flaw than a skillset weakness, consider reading books, taking courses, or practicing other self-development actions to rework your weaknesses into strengths.

If you have a concept of perfection, you will always be disappointed in yourself. Perfection isn't attainable. Not one person on this planet is close to perfect. All you can do is try your best. But even then, there are so many variables you can never predict.

If you can honestly tell yourself that you're trying your best, let that be enough. You can change your plans along the way, but there's nothing wrong with it not being exactly as you planned initially. People who strive for perfection often fail to launch, start, or take any action. And at the end of the day, it's the failure to start that prevents you from getting out of your own way. So!

Get out of your own way by replacing negative thoughts with positive ones. Negativity can spread through the mind fast and affect your performance. Any time you have a negative idea, say the polar opposite belief in your mind. Do this every time it happens.

You'll retrain your brain to think more optimistically. Often when we think negatively, our brain creates pathways to make negative thinking more common. Fortunately, a positive thinking practice can make happier thoughts more common too. Stay focus…

Focus on milestones towards the ultimate goal of wealth creation. You see your big goals will seem particularly hard to achieve at times. The struggle or the amount of time involved shouldn't deter you.

Create milestones along the way. Break down that ultimate goal into manageable pieces. As you see the progress you make, it will help you stay focused on the ultimate goal. Even with a solid plan of action, there will be challenges that get in your way. Don't let them hold you back or discourage you.

Conclusion

The journey of focusing and getting out of your own way is all about taking the right steps with self-confidence. You do deserve all the success and happiness you want for your life. You will accomplish anything you set for yourself. Now, get out there and take that first step. You are a creator of wealth.